A5

English G 21

Klassenarbeitstrainer

für Schülerinnen und Schüler

Lösungen und Lerntipps

Cornelsen

Lösungen A

LISTENING

01 1 A high school photo competition

(...)

Mrs Miller	You each have your cards in front of you. For a start, I'd just like to start; my personal favourite is number 3.
Mr Bush	You're kidding!
Lesley	Really?
Mrs Miller	Yeah.
Mr Bush	Number three?
Mrs Miller	Yeah, I find this use of contrast fantastic, I think the colours are beautiful, a beautiful lonely pier, stretching out to the horizon. You could almost be walking along it.
Mr Bush	I mean I guess you could, could imagine yourself sitting on the edge of the wharf and putting your legs in the water, but for me it's not really Australia.
Lesley	Australia, exactly, that's what I was thinking.
Mr Bush	You think the same?
Lesley	It's not really Australia because, well it is Australia, but it's not, it doesn't say Australia to me.
Mr Bush	It could be anywhere.
Lesley	Exactly, it could be like the Caribbean or ...
Mrs Miller	It could be anywhere, it could be anywhere but we don't want to necessarily fall into these clichés as well.
Mr Bush	What about number five?
Lesley	Oh you like it 'cause you're a sailor, Mr Bush.
Mrs Miller	Yeah you like sailing Mr Bush.
Mr Bush	OK, OK, but I mean it's a brilliant image, I mean.
Lesley	It is a great image but once again that could be, I don't know, in Spain or something, I mean I know we don't want to go cliché Australia but ...
Mr Bush	OK, OK.
Mrs Miller	The colours certainly are beautiful in that picture ... the blue is fabulous ...
Mr Bush	Number two is for me a bit like a postcard really.
Lesley	Yeah, I agree.
Mr Bush	I mean, just look at those rocks, the way they just jut out of the sea, it's fantastic, it's, it's a great image. But, the thing is, the rocks, and the beach and ... this is the Twelve Apostles, it's like a postcard photo. I mean, I know that place, it looks like that ...
Mrs Miller	Number two, I mean how many times have we seen that photo before?
Lesley	Yeah that's true.
Mr Bush	And, what about number one Lesley, what do you think of that?
Lesley	I like number one and number six.
Mrs Miller	I like number one too.
Lesley	Yeah?
Mrs Miller	I like number one, this new view of, of the skyline at night, I was, yeah it's beautiful.

Mr Bush	Is that from the North shore do you think?
Lesley	No, I think that's from the Eastern shore because the Harbour Bridge is on the, on the right, but I want to talk about number six if I can because, I mean, that for me is, is such a brilliant shot because you can see faintly in the background the Sydney Harbour Bridge and then in the foreground is all this movement.
Mrs Miller	You're right and, you just, it's, the simplicity of children playing is really nice, isn't it?
Lesley	Yeah, so it's fun, peacefulness, summer.
Mrs Miller	Also it's not cliché; we haven't seen that picture before.
Lesley	Exactly! Yeah, I don't know, I, I really like number six, six or one for me.
Mr Bush	Well, I'd say one is out of it but number, number four is for me a typical, um, look at that white sand, and this, the foliation, the green leaves ...
Lesley	Yeah, but there's no movement in it. Do you know what I mean?
Mr Bush	The clouds, the clouds ...
Lesley	So what do you think? Number six?
Mr Bush	Well, I mean ...
Lesley	Number six, number six ...
Mr Bush	You're speaking from the students' viewpoint, so ...
Mrs Miller	I'm personally torn between number six, number three and number one.
Lesley	OK, and I like number six, so that's two for number six ...
Mr Bush	Alright, alright, alright, two to one ... Anyway, I can, I can see what you're saying about number six, it's just, you know, it's just this darkness underneath is a little bit ... anyway, but I could live with number six.
Lesley	Yeah? Great. – Number six?
Mrs Miller	Yeah, good.
Mr Bush	So, when will you tell the kids?
Mrs Miller	Well, I'll let the kids know in assembly tomorrow. (...)

a)

A2, B3, C6, D1, E4, F5

Picture D shows the Harbour Bridge but is not as beautiful as the other photo of it so it must be number one.

Picture A shows the rocks so it has to be number two.

In picture B you can see a sunset, so it is number three.

Picture E shows a quiet sea, so it must be number four.

Picture F must be number five because it has something to do with sailing.

Picture C shows the Harbour Bridge again but there is also movement in this picture, that's why I think it is number six.

b)

Mögliche Lösung:

I would have chosen picture three because I love sunsets. The sunset in this picture is one of the most beautiful ones I have ever seen. It really makes me want to go to Australia as soon as I get the chance.

02 2 An interview for the school radio station

Steve Hello there fellow students, teachers and anyone else who's listening. This is Steve broadcasting live from Caroline Chisholm High's radio station, and in the studio with me today we have Maya. Hello Maya!

Maya Hi Steve!

Steve Um, Maya is this year's winner of the photo competition. Congratulations!

Maya Thank you.

Steve So how old are you, Maya?

Maya I'm 16, I'm in year 9.

Steve Year 9? OK, and, um, is this the first time that you've participated in the competition?

Maya No, no, I was in it, um, a couple of years ago. I didn't get anywhere the other time so this is the second time, yep.

Steve OK, and what was the photograph you took a couple of years ago?

Maya Erm, I think it was something of my family, yeah.

Steve Oh really?

Maya Yeah.

Steve So you've been taking photos for quite some time?

Maya Yeah, I started ten years ago when I was six ...

Steve Wow!

Maya Yeah, I got a camera for my birthday and, um, and yeah and I started on my birthday.

Steve Yeah wow.

Maya So I just started taking photos and yeah ...

Steve And you haven't stopped since.

Maya Not really no.

Steve Wow, so, um, tell us, the photo that you took, um, tell us a little bit about the photo or what inspired you to take it.

Maya Well, like I said, the other time I was in the competition I took a photograph, photograph of my family, and so I've always, I've never really liked like touristy shots, it's like it's not really, they're not my best photographs ...

Steve Sure.

Maya My best photographs are always the things like, photographs of my family, people that I knew really well that I could get closer to and so this time I just walked around a lot in my neighbourhood and looked at places that I knew really well and, um, and yeah, and so ...

Steve And, and this was it?

Maya Yeah, I just got lucky with the light I think and yeah ...

Steve Excellent, um, just for the people who maybe haven't seen the photograph do you wanna explain a little bit about the, where you were, or kind of the context of the photograph?

Maya Well, yeah there's a park and it's really open, green space, um, and it looks out over the harbour, you can see the Harbour Bridge in the distance, but there's a, in the centreground of the photograph there's a kids' playground and there's a slide going down one direction and swings on the other one and somebody's swinging right the way back ... um, so that it's kind of opposite direction from the slide so there's a contrast and the sun's setting behind it so ...

Steve Yeah, and for those of you who haven't seen it, it really is a splendid and beautiful photo. Um, so tell me how did you feel when the art teacher announced that you were this year's winner?

Maya Oh my god, I was so excited! I was just like, oh my god! 'cause I didn't get anywhere the other time and I was like "wow" and my friends were like "cool, yeah, good one!", you know so ...

Steve Excellent, excellent ... And for those of us who don't know, can you tell us what the prize is?

Maya Um, it's a really good camera, high quality camera, much better than the one I've got, the, um, the yeah the pixel rate is really good and yeah really good lens, so I'm looking forward to trying it out!

Steve Wow, excellent, alright, well thanks a lot Maya, and thanks a lot everybody else for joining us! See you soon.

Maya Bye!

a)

1 She has already participated in a photo competition.

2 She started taking pictures ten years ago.

3 Her best photographs show her family and friends.

4 She thinks the light was very good.

5 She was very excited when the art teacher announced her name.

b)

Sentence	True	False	Correction
Maya started taking photos when she was five.		✔	She started taking pictures ten years ago. / She started taking pictures when she was six.
She wasn't successful in her first competition.	✔		
Maya planned to take a picture of her favourite kids' playground.		✔	She didn't plan to take the photo, she just walked around a lot in her neighbourhood and looked at places that she knew very well.
Maya likes touristy photos very much.		✔	She doesn't like touristy photos. Her best photographs are those of her family and other people she knows very well.
The prize is a very good camera.	✔		

MEDIATION

A photo competition

1 Man muss das Foto zusammen mit einer Beschreibung und Bildunterschrift und seinem Namen, seiner Adresse und Telefonnummer einsenden.

2 Einsendeschluss ist der 10. Oktober um Mitternacht. Jeder über 16 Jahre darf teilnehmen. Das Foto muss den Namen und eine Bildüberschrift tragen. Das Foto muss mindestens 1 MB groß sein. Jeder darf nur ein Foto pro Monat einsenden.

3 Man kann eine Kamera gewinnen, die $ 500 wert ist.

4 Ein Foto wird nicht zugelassen, wenn es mit der Post geschickt wird.

5 Das Foto wird in der nächsten Ausgabe des Magazins zusammen mit dem Namen des Fotografen veröffentlicht.

LANGUAGE

1 WORDS Melanie reports from Australia

On the farm I met Joey, the 16-year-old son of the family. When I first saw him, I thought he was gorgeous. I thought that he would be very serious because he was showing me my work on the farm, but in fact he spent all his time laughing and making jokes. To start with I couldn't help laughing with him, but because he was my instructor, I became nervous and began to freak out.

One day he told me about his favourite hobby: he and his mate like riding their dirt bikes on dirt roads through the Australian outback. Sometimes they see animals like emus and koalas. That's quite impressive, isn't it? Because the climate in Australia is so hot and sunny. Joey and his friend have to put on sunscreen before they go out even when they're wearing special clothes. The hole in the ozone layer lets dangerous ultraviolet rays pass into the atmosphere. Even if you're sitting in the shade, you have to be careful because the sun is still dangerous. It's a really serious problem and a lot of Australians do develop skin cancer.

After they go for their bike rides, Joey and his mate like to go for a barbecue down at the beach and they invite other friends too. The Aussies even have beach parties on Christmas Day! That must be a really unique experience!

2 Tricky translations

Last Friday was the big day: our date! We met in front of the farmhouse. I wore my best dress and Joey looked great. He offered to carry my jacket for me – that was very sweet! Joey wanted to drive to the restaurant but the car was broken so we had to wait for another hour and then go by bus. He made a short call and asked his mate if he could help him repair the car the next day. While we were waiting for the bus, we laughed a lot. That was a good start! When we arrived at the restaurant, we took our seats and the waiter brought the menu. It was very difficult to choose because everything sounded great. It took us ages to decide and I needed Joey to help me, but we finally ordered. We talked a lot during dinner and Joey was so funny. I have to say that when I first met him, I didn't really like him. He laughed at me because I didn't know how to ride a horse. And then, just three days ago, I got very angry with him because he was acting like my big brother and correcting me all the time. But during our date he was lovely.
It was the chef himself who brought us our dinner! It was fantastic.
When the waiter had taken the p lates away and we had finished our drinks, we decided to do something else. I thought we should go to the cinema, and Joey agreed. The film was very scary and I was happy that Joey was with me because he's very tall so I wasn't afraid in the dark streets after the film. When we got home, he kissed me good night. It was a fantastic date and I hope we'll do it again very soon!

3 GRAMMAR Melanie's time in Australia

Mögliche Lösungen:

On January 15th Melanie packed her bag.

Before she arrived in Australia / went to Australia / went to Sydney / travelled to Australia, she had received a visa.

After Melanie had bought a ticket she did a boat tour in Sydney. / Before Melanie did a boat tour, she had bought a ticket.

Melanie is now feeding the cows.

Joey rides his dirt bike every day.

Before Melanie was allowed to drive a dirt bike, she had had to learn the Australian road rules / she had practised for the exam.

MEDIATION

Welcome to Queensland!

You Schaut mal, was ich über Queensland im Internet gefunden habe!

Father Nicht schlecht ... Kann man dort Tiere beobachten?

You Na klar, man kann eine Safari unternehmen oder Wale beobachten. (2P)

Mother Ich bin ja eher für etwas Geschichte ...

You Das ist auch kein Problem. Es gibt viele Museen und Ausstellungen über die Kunst und die Geschichte der Aborigines. (2P)

Father Gibt es auch etwas Spannenderes?

You Sicher! Wir können an Abenteuertouren teilnehmen oder in einen Freizeitpark gehen. (2P)

Mother Ich würde ja auch gerne ein bisschen einkaufen gehen ...

You Das kannst du auch. Es gibt viele Einkaufszentren und Märkte. (2P)

Father Wie sieht es denn mit einer Unterkunft aus?

You Wir können ein ruhiges Apartment auf dem Land mieten oder in einem Strandhotel in der Stadt wohnen. (2P)

Father Worauf warten wir dann noch? Auf geht's nach Australien!

WRITING

Feeling homesick

Mögliche Lösung:

Dear Aurélie,

I was very sorry to hear that you're not feeling so good at the moment.

When I arrived here, I was very lonely too. I missed my family terribly! But it got better. (1P) Are you allowed to go out in the evenings? Maybe you could meet some friends and go to the cinema or have a pizza somewhere. (3P) I do that once a week and it really helps me. (1P) At the beginning it was a bit difficult to get in contact with other young people. Maybe your family knows some teenagers your age? Just ask them out! (3P)

I think my life here is a bit different because the next city is a long way away and I have a lot of work to do on the farm. But Melbourne probably has a lot of things to offer! You should be open to trying new things, Australia is very exciting! (4P)

It sounds like you've made a good start anyway: I was really interested to hear about your exciting trip to the outback last week. (2P) Did you like it? (1P) I haven't done that yet but I would really love to go! I think it's great that your family organizes such interesting trips for you. Try to enjoy them and I'm sure you'll feel better very soon. (3P)

Can't wait to read your reply. All the best! (1P)

Love, (1P)

Mel

SPEAKING

Bushfire!

Mögliche Lösung:

The table shows the different causes of bushfires in Victoria. It compares the numbers of bushfires to each other (1P) and gives information about the reasons for the fires, the average number of fires each year and the percentage of total fires. (3P) Bushfires start for quite a number of different reasons. (1P) Some of them are natural, some of them are manmade. (2P) Lightning causes the largest percentage of fires in Australia, while machinery and exhausts cause the lowest. (2P) The statistics also tell us that, apart from the fires started by lightning, most fires are started deliberately. (1P) If you add the agricultural reasons to the fires started by cigarettes, you have almost three quarters of all bushfires. (2P)
Only one quarter (26 %) of all bushfires are started by nature, e.g. lightning. (1P) All the others are started by people, which I think is very surprising. (1P) So that shows that the majority of fires could be prevented. (1P) To conclude, you can say that these statistics show that people should be more careful about the bush. (1P)

Lösungen B

READING

School of the Air Alice Springs

a)

	Right	Wrong	Not given
1 Children in the outback are less active than city children.		✔	
2 There is no homework at the School of the Air.			✔
3 Outback children have special skills and know how to survive in the outback.	✔		
4 The School of the Air provides lessons for about 120 students.	✔		
5 Most of them travel a long distance to school every day.		✔	
6 School of the Air students get better grades than students at normal schools.			✔

b)

Mögliche Lösungen:

1 The students live too far away from each other and from a normal school building.

2 They don't have to come to school, they are educated via the internet.

3 The students learn how to study by themselves and are very well organized.

4 They go to a boarding school.

LANGUAGE

1 WORDS Explaining words

Mögliche Lösungen:

Word	Explanation
independent	An independent person is someone who can live on his or her own without help from others.
suntan	If you spend time in the sun, you will develop this.
useful	It can be ~ to have a map when you visit a city you've never been to before.
conclusion	At the end of an essay you write a conclusion.
mattress	When you are in bed, you lie on this.
jealous	If your brother thinks that your parents love you more than him, this is how he feels.
poison	You might die if you eat or drink this.

2 GRAMMAR Students at the School of the Air

Interviewer Why do you learn with the School of the Air?

Boy My parents wanted me to learn with the School of the Air. There's no school near our house, so they thought it was a good idea for me.

Interviewer Can you describe school life to me and the listeners?

Boy Yes, of course. The computer is in our living room. We communicate via the internet, and the first thing I do in the morning is say hello to my classmates. Sometimes my little sister is still in the room, so I have to tell her to leave. Then, usually our teacher wants us to read our homework.
Sometimes my father helps me to understand mathematical problems. (help – understand) He wants me to work harder at school. But that's quite difficult when there's nobody around to check if you're doing your school work.

Interviewer So being a student at the School of the Air is not always easy. Let's see what the next student has to say. Thanks for the interview!

Boy No worries!

3 GRAMMAR A new student at the School of the Air

I don't know / I'm not sure who to talk to on the first morning.

I don't know / I'm not sure what to say to my new classmates.

I don't know / I'm not sure when to do my homework.

I don't know / I'm not sure how to hand in the assignments.

I don't know / I'm not sure where to get my student ID from.

4 GRAMMAR The life of a School of the Air student

1 There is a lot of work to do over the weekend.
2 There are different assignments to complete.
3 We have a teacher to take care of the new students.
4 During the break I go and see my mum in the kitchen to have a cup of tea.
5 I'm happy that there is no uniform to wear.
6 I am the first person in my life to come to Australia as an exchange student.
7 We had nobody to ask for help.
8 At the beginning there are a lot of new things to learn.

WRITING

Australian Aborigines

Mögliche Lösung:

Aborigines have been living in Australia for a very long time.

Art has always been an important means of expression for them. 40,000 years ago they developed the oldest rock art in the world.

In the nineteenth century, European settlers came to Australia. They thought Aboriginal culture was primitive and they did not respect it. They forced the Aborigines to move from the land. Aborigines who did not go were very often killed. As a consequence the number of Aborigines reduced. Aborigines were discriminated against and did not get the right to vote until 1963. A very sad fact is that until the 1970s, Aboriginal children were taken away from their families and had to live with white Australians.

Today, Australia's population is more than 20 million, and only about 2 % of those are Aborigines. Some of them still move around within a limited area and live in tribes. The oldest members of the tribes make decisions for the others.

Today the most serious problems are discrimination and poverty. Many drink too much alcohol and they very often do not have a job.

SPEAKING

I can tell you more

a)

Mögliche Lösungen:

A Hi! When did you arrive?

B I arrived 10 days ago.

A Wow, that sounds good. My name is Leon by the way. We arrived yesterday.

B Hi, I'm John. You're German, right?

A Yes, I come from Frankfurt am Main, that's in the west of Germany. Where are you from?

B I'm from Alice Springs, Northern Territory, Australia. Have you been camping before?

A Yes, we go camping every year. It's our first time here. What about you?

B I love camping, too. It's our third time here. And the weather has always been great.

A Do you know where the pool is?

B Sure, it's near the entrance, we can walk over there if you like.

A Maybe later. What about a disco or a café? Is there a nice place to go in the evenings?

B There's a nice café at the campsite it's just opposite the supermarket. And there's a disco every Friday evening just outside the campsite. It's great. It's only about five minutes' walk.

A I'd like to go to the beach. Is it far?

B I want to go to the beach in half an hour. We can go together if you like.

A Good idea. I'll go and get my towel. See you soon / in 30 minutes, John.

B See you!

b)

A Hi! When did you arrive?

B I arrived 10 days ago.

A Wow, that sounds good. My name is Laura by the way. We arrived yesterday.

B Hi, I'm Jenny. You're German, right?

A Yes, I come from Chemnitz, that's in the east of Germany. Where are you from?

B I'm from Cardiff in Wales. Have you been camping before?

A Yes, we go camping every year, but this is our first time at this campsite. What about you?

B It's our third time here. But this year the weather has been bad so far, so much rain! And it's been really cold. I hate camping. What about you?

A I really hate camping too. I'd prefer a holiday in a hotel. And you?

B Me too. You can relax in your room or in the hotel and if the weather is bad, there are always things to do in a hotel.

A Where would you like to go?

B I'd love to go to different places every year, I want to get to know the big European cities like Paris, Barcelona or Vienna. Where would you like to go?

A I really like holidays at the sea because I love swimming and I like eating fish!

B Listen, I'd love to have an ice-cream. What about you? We could go and get one from the shop.

A Good idea. I'll just get my money. See you in a minute, Jenny.

B See you!

Lösungen A

READING

Different jobs for different people

Mögliche Lösung:

1 You will earn more for sales in the call centre and you will earn more as you gain experience as an apple picker.

2 You don't need to have experience in any of these jobs. / Experience isn't required anywhere.

3 They offer jobs as sales assistants and stock-taking jobs.

4 You have to be prepared to work very hard.

5 You need to speak English fluently and be confident.

WRITING

Applying for a job

a)

Mögliche Lösung:

From: eve.flanders@googlemail.com

To: staff@callyou.co.uk (1P)

Re: Application for a job as a call centre agent (1P)

Dear Sir or Madam, (1P)

I am writing to you about your advertisement in the Springfield News of February 21st. I would like to work as a call centre agent. (2P)

I am 16 years old and already have some valuable work experience. I have worked for our school's newspaper for two years now. I am responsible for selling it to the students at my school. (3P) Besides this, I have sales experience working in my father's boutique "Leftorium" in Springfield. (2P) I sell the latest fashions in the shop to our customers. (1P) I also answer the phone and deal with orders made by phone. (2P)

I love talking to other people, and my spoken and written English is fluent. (2P) I attach my recent school certificates and my CV to this e-mail. (2P)

Thank you for your time. I look forward to hearing from you. (1P)

Yours faithfully, (1P)

Eve Flanders

Eve Flanders

Phone: ++44-2866-7180965

E-mail: eve.flanders@googlemail.com (1P)

b)

Mögliche Lösung:

7 Glasgow Road
Bristol BS15 3LA (1P)

Alice Spring
St. John's Residential Care Home
4 New Garden Street
Bristol BS1 3AD (1P)

4 November 2011 (1P)

Dear Ms Spring (1P)

I am writing about your advertisement in The Bristol Times from 2 November. I would like to apply for the job at St. John's Residential Care Home. (2P)

I am 16 years old and have very good IT skills. As well as using the computer at home. I have learned a great deal about IT at school. Last term I organized an extracurricular group after school for younger students to help them with their research for school projects on the internet. I have also taught my grandparents to write e-mails and how to download their favourite music, so I have experience in working with older people too. (8P)

I could start after Christmas and am available on Monday, Wednesday or Thursday afternoons. (2P)

Please find my CV with this letter. (2P)

Thank you for your time. I look forward to hearing from you. (1P)

Yours sincerely (1P)
Sue Evans
Sue Evans

LANGUAGE

1 WORDS Jobs

a)

Mögliche Lösungen:

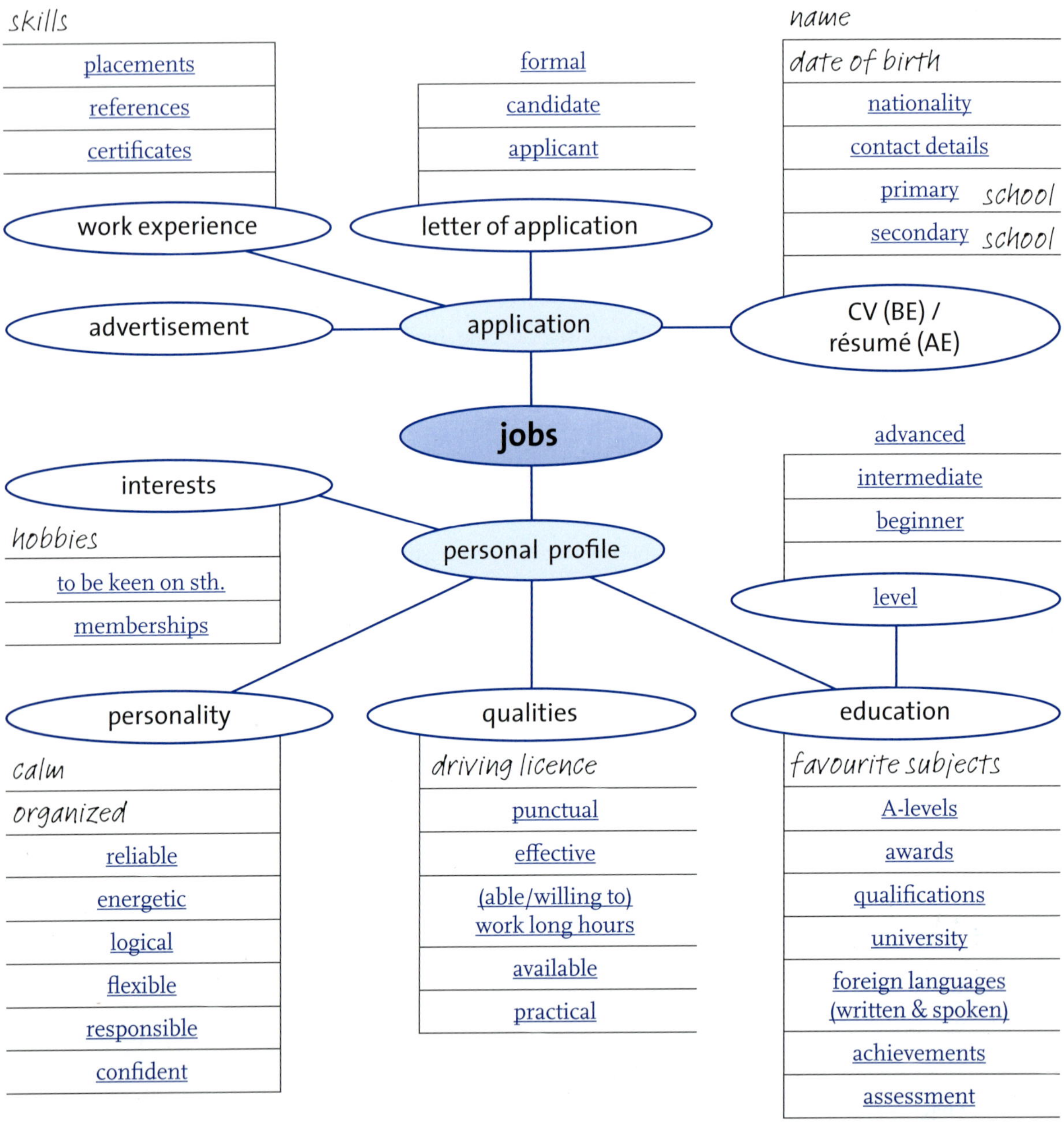

b)

Mögliche Lösungen:

I always enclose any references I have when I send an application.

Don't forget to give your contact details.

I am available on Mondays, Tuesdays and Fridays.

I am a reliable person, you can trust me.

2 WORDS Nigel's nightmare of getting a job

1 Sometimes I have the feeling that it is impossible to get the perfect job.

2 So far I have been unlucky in finding a job.

3 I felt very uncomfortable at my last interview.

4 It would be impolite to tell the manager that you think his tie looks awful.

5 You take a big risk if you apply for a job and your CV is inaccurate.

3 GRAMMAR This is me!

My name is Timmy and I am good at playing football and listening to other people's problems. At least this is what people say … . I like going to the cinema with my best friend Tony. Hanging around with friends from school is great fun! Leading a healthy life is also important for me. I stay fit by doing lots of sports and eating all my vegetables. I am keen on riding my scooter. I'm always very serious about environmental issues without getting involved in politics. After I leave school I want to study law and become a judge. Well, what else …? Ah, yes. What I don't like is doing homework. It ruins my whole day, I can tell you.

4 WORDS Translating „Möglichkeit"

1 Have you had the chance/opportunity to contact the job agency yet?

2 There are a number of ways to apply for a job.

3 Have you thought of the possibility of asking for a job in the shop?

4 The chances of getting a job without an interview are very small indeed.

5 There is no way of getting to this place without a car.

6 We have the possibility of going to Madame Tussaud's when we are in London.

5 GRAMMAR Things the employer tells you

2 You shouldn't mind getting your hands dirty.

3 This job is good if you like getting to know / to get to know new people.

4 Asking other workers is helpful.

5 Taking too many toilet breaks is not appreciated.

6 Making personal phone calls can get you into trouble.

7 Being late for work can also cause problems.

8 Avoid having long lunch breaks.

9 Do you fancy working abroad?

10 I can imagine sending you to our Australian branch.

STUDY SKILLS

Getting a scholarship for the USA

Lerntipp Einen Lebenslauf schreiben

Zusätzlich kannst du ein Bewerbungsschreiben für das Stipendium formulieren, um Bewerbungsschreiben zu üben.

Dein Text enthält ...	Punkte
1. personal information (name, age, city)	2
2. personal statement	4
3. schools	2
4. work experience	3
5. hobbies and interests	4
6. special knowledge, awards	2
7. extracurricular activities and qualifications	4

SPEAKING

03 An assessment centre – Part 1

Mc Fly Good afternoon, my name is Pete Mc Fly. I'm a manager at Boxcom and Partners. We've received your application and would like to get to know you better. Could you come into our office either next Tuesday, 14th of April or Friday, 17th of April? Please get back to us at 0151 4807978. Thank you and goodbye.

04 Now you

Mc Fly Boxcom and Partners. You're speaking to Pete Mc Fly. How can I help you?

You Hello, my name is ... Thank you for your message. Could you tell me if it is a job interview or an assessment centre?

Mc Fly It's an assessment centre.

You I'm not quite sure what an assessment centre is. Do you think you could give me some more information?

Mc Fly Well, it's sort of an interview. There'll be other participants there and you'll work on a task together. Some of my colleagues and I will be watching how you work together and which role you take in the group.

You Have I got that right? If I participate successfully in the assessment centre, I'll then be invited to a job interview?

Mc Fly Right. I understand you're nervous about the assessment centre, but I can assure you, you don't have to be! Just be yourself! Do you think you could make it next Tuesday?

You Yes, of course. Could you tell me the exact address?

Mc Fly Oh, yes. I almost forgot. We'll meet in my office, 32 Stratford Street, second floor. Ask at reception, and they'll guide you through the building. Do you have any more questions about the assessment centre?

You OK, no problem, I know exactly how to get there. I don't have any other questions.

Mc Fly That's wonderful. So I'll see you next Tuesday at ten then. We should be finished by four. I look forward to it.

You Thank you very much.

Mc Fly You're welcome. Bye.

LISTENING

05 Are you happy with your job?

Terry Good morning and welcome to today's show, Radio Today. I'd like to give a very warm welcome to all of our listeners out there, and err, we have a themed week on the topic "Are you happy with your job?" And every morning between 10 and 11, I'll be interviewing a different person on this topic. And today I'm interviewing Alice who has her own shop. – Erm, Alice, have you always been happy with your job?

Alice Err, no Terry I haven't actually, erm, I'm thirty years old now, and yeah my career's going well now. I've got my own boutique, but when I was sixteen, I just didn't know what to do after school. So first of all I just started working at my father's shop, a radio and TV shop, erm, and I just, you know, first of all I, I didn't like radios or TVs, erm, I wasn't interested in the topic, but also I was just working with my family all the time, and that just was not for me. So I stopped working for my father and moved out of the family home and what followed was a bit of a weird period, to be honest.

Terry So how did you find out which job was best for you then?

Alice Well after I'd moved out I started work in a supermarket, and that really gave me a lot of time to think about what I was really good at. You know, my interests, what I really wanted to do, and I talked to a lot of people, that really helped. And I finally applied for a job in a boutique and became a successful shop assistant, erm, and I found out that the manager was happy with my work and that sort of egged me on even further.

Terry And, erm, something else, are your working hours important to you?

Alice Well, erm, now that I am own boss, erm, yes working hours are important for me definitely, but you know after seven years of just doing courses, and, and thinking about what I wanted to do, I decided I don't want to be a millionaire, but I want to be my own boss, so you know, I don't have many holidays, I, I close the shop for three weeks in the late autumn and I have a relaxing holiday then, that is important to me, erm but I am so happy in my job, it's so fulfilling that I don't really mind the working hours because I've sort of made my hobby my job, if you see what I mean.

Terry Yes, yes. Okay Alice, thank you very much indeed.

Alice That was a pleasure Terry, thank you for having me.

a)

Sentence	True	False	Why
1 Alice hasn't always been happy with her job, but her career is going well now.	✔		
2 Alice doesn't like her job because she doesn't have much free time anymore.		✔	False. She doesn't mind not having many holidays.
3 Alice knew from the start what she wanted to do after school.		✔	False. She didn't know what to do after school.
4 After school Alice started to work at her father's computer shop.		✔	False. She started to work at her father's radio and TV shop.
5 Alice worked in a supermarket and thought about her interests.	✔		
6 Alice has a boutique with one of her friends now.		✔	False. She has her own shop.
7 Alice has made her hobby her job.	✔		

06 *Terry* Hello, good morning, I'd like to welcome all of our listeners out there to today's programme, Radio Today. I'm Terry Cooper and today on the show, I'll be interviewing Harry. He's only 28 but he's already written a book about how to get the best job. – Good morning, Harry.

Harry Err, good morning, Terry.

Terry Um, could you just tell us first of all, how did your career start exactly?

Harry Oh right, erm, well, erm, when I first left school I started working in a careers office, and I was doing secretarial jobs, erm, for about three years. Then I got the chance to do some special training to become a careers advisor and I also did this job for a few years and I actually advised hundreds of young people, some of them who wrote me letters to thank me for my help, and without boasting I still get some letters off [besser wäre *from*] these people. Erm, after a while I decided that I wanted to help more young people, so I started working part-time so I would have time to write this book, and this book is all about helping young people find the best job for them.

Terry Right, and how did you the idea of writing the book?

Harry After working with so many young people, I started seeing that ... two people aren't the same, every single person is individual, so, erm, I started thinking of different ways that people can find the perfect job for themselves.

Terry OK, OK that's very interesting, and, erm, what was the most important step in your career?

Harry Erm, I think it was just getting out there and finding some work because that's how I found out what I personally liked to do.

Terry And have you stopped working as a career [besser wäre *careers*] advisor?

Harry Err, I still work a little bit, I work part-time but I do focus mainly on the book and going out there, doing talks and advising young people.

Terry OK, what information can readers find in your book, and, and what won't they find?

Harry Well, err, the book, it's basically a guide that helps you through the jungle of job applications.

Terry OK ...

Harry Erm, it's a practical book, erm, it has lots of funny pictures and it also has cartoons in there to make you laugh because what I found with young people is they don't just wanna read and read and read, they need something that focuses them and, erm, something that's interesting.

Terry OK, and what won't they find in the book?

Harry Well, like I just mentioned, they won't just find pages and pages of information that will make them go to sleep, erm, they won't find things that are telling them that is the one particular way to do things.

Terry Right, so it's lively and engaging.

Harry It's lively, it's engaging, well I hope it's lively and engaging and, erm, the response like I said that I've had off [besser wäre *from*] young people has been very positive.

Terry And what makes you happy in your job above all else?

Harry Erm, the best thing for me in my job is making other people happy, and getting people, and giving them the advice, and pushing them down the road for their perfect job.

Terry Great, OK Harry we'll have a little break here with some music and after the break we come back and we'll listen to Harry's tips.

b)

1a), 2b), 3c), 4b), 5a)

06 *Terry* And, err, we're back after that little break there, err, back here with Harry, who, as I say is only 28 but has already written a book about how to get that, err, the best job, and, err, so Harry, what are your tips?

Harry Well, err, the 'shoulds' of getting a good job that you really like, err, are you should take time to find out what you're really interested in, and find out your strengths.

Terry Right.

Harry In the book there is a game which helps you to match your interests and strengths with different jobs. Find out your other skills by volunteer work, or by doing work experience. Talk to other people about their jobs whenever possible. Apply for jobs. Practise interviews! Every job interview is practice for the next one.

Terry Right, right.

Harry So, get more confident talking about yourself. The 'should nots' are, well, don't worry if you don't get a job straight away, but just don't sit at home waiting for the phone to ring, you should volunteer for work, or, I don't know, try to learn a foreign language. Do training, if possible and don't think that a good job is always a job which pays you a lot of money.

Terry Hmm, alright Harry, thank you very much indeed, that's, that's great advice.

Harry Thank you.

Terry I'm sure all of our young people out there will very much appreciate that, and, err, get out there and buy that book and give it a good read, and, err, and take, err, Harry's, err, tips and advice on board.

Harry Available at all good bookstores at £7.99.

Terry Of course, and well worth the money. Thank you very much indeed Harry.

c)

Shoulds	Should nots
take time to find out what you're really interested in	don't worry if you don't get a job straight away
find out your strengths	don't sit at home waiting for the phone to ring
volunteer for work	don't think that a good job is always a job which pays you a lot of money
try to learn a foreign language	
find out your skills by volunteer work or by doing work experience	
talk to other people about their jobs	
apply for jobs	
practise interviews	
get more confident talking about yourself	

LANGUAGE

1 WORDS The downside of being rich

It all started because I wanted to impress my classmates at school. I have always been interested in computers and games, so I decided to focus on creating websites for companies. At my uncle's birthday party I met a guy who was successful in that kind of work, and he advised me to concentrate on special designs which nobody had ever done before. I was determined to start my own business and so I decided not to go to university.
I told my parents that it wasn't necessary for me to study and to my great surprise they stayed calm. The more pages I created, the more my ambition grew and my determination to achieve more. I was responsible for my own projects! My little business became very successful and I soon needed employees. My faith in myself increased and I became more confident. I thought I could make my fortune in this business. However, within a few months I lost something which I had never enjoyed as much as I could: I realized I wasn't a child anymore. I was leading the stressful life of a greedy adult!

2 GRAMMAR Stop being lazy and get a job

I remember talking to my teacher about applications last year. He told me to stop making so many mistakes in my application letters. I tried really hard, but he still always found a lot of mistakes in the applications I showed him. I'll never forget listening to all the feedback he gave me. For practice, I tried to write as many applications as I could. And I even stopped playing football with my friends or going to the cinema with them after school. I also improved my CV. One day I sent an application to a company. I was very nervous and in the meantime I even tried doing yoga to calm myself down. One week later I got a letter and now I have a job interview, I'm so happy! I mustn't forget to call my mother after the interview and I must remember to say thank you to my teacher.

3 GRAMMAR We want you!

Are you interested in earning some extra money?
Are you used to teaching your favourite subject to other students?
Are you interested in writing exercises?
Are you good at explaining ideas and concepts?
Are you keen on helping younger students from your school?
Are you tired of spending afternoons alone?
Do you dream of being a teacher?

MEDIATION

A job for your exchange partner

Pete Well, this is the advert I found in the newspaper. What kind of job is it exactly?

You They are looking for someone to help out in the tourist information in Stuttgart.

Pete And what do I have to do? *(three things)*

You You have to welcome American tourists at the airport and give them a flyer about Stuttgart. At the tourist information, you will have to pass on any English questions to our trained members of staff.

Pete That sounds good to me. But don't I have to know the area for this job?

You No, not really. You don't have to know the area. / It doesn't say so in the advert.

Pete But what skills do I need? *(three things)*

You You should be self-confident and speak English fluently. Besides, you should be punctual and reliable.

Pete When do I have to work?

You Your working hours are from Monday to Saturday from 9 am until 6.30 pm.

Pete But I'm only here for the summer holidays.

You That's OK. It's only a summer job.

Pete OK then. How can I apply for it? *(two things)*

You You can either visit the tourist information directly and ask for Mrs Eigel. Or you can call her on 0711 – 34 56 78.

SPEAKING

An assessment centre – Part 2

Mögliche Lösungen:

Personal information	Name: Daniel Förster
	Age: 15
	City in which you live: Stuttgart
Education	2002–2006 Max-und-Moritz-Grundschule (Primary School) 2006–now Klaus-Peter-Bärbelmann-Schule (Secondary School)
What your interests are (should have to do something with the job)	Computers Creating websites Handball
What your skills are (should have something to do with the job)	Good at creating websites (member of school club) Helping other people Working together in a team
Why you applied for the job	Like creating websites and am interested in modern technology Used to working in a team
What makes you the best person for the job	I already have some experience in creating websites and in software programming. I have already sold some websites to companies in my home town

Lerntipp **Sprechen üben**

Wenn du deinen Vortrag aufgenommen und anhand der Lösungen kontrolliert hast oder von einer zuhörenden Person eine Rückmeldung bekommen hast, solltest du in deinem Lernheft vermerken, worauf du beim nächsten Mal verstärkt achten wirst. Wiederhole dann diese Übung nach einiger Zeit noch einmal.

Bewertung und Punkte

Deine Tabelle enthält …	Punkte
1. personal information (name, age, city)	2
2. information about your education	2
3. your interests	2
4. your skills	2
5. reasons for your application	4
6. reasons why you're the best	4

LISTENING

07 I love my city!

Abdel Hello, my name is Abdel and I come from Joburg in South Africa. I love my city, it is a very nice place, it is warm and it's sunny. On the weekends I like to make [besser wäre *have*] parties and go out, this is something that we do quite a lot here in South Africa. The city does get crowded quite a lot, particularly from [besser wäre *with*] tourists, but I appreciate that the tourist industry is very, very important to South Africa. This was very, very clear to us in 2010 when millions of people came to our country for the FIFA World Cup. We had a great time and we were very, very proud. We have a big problem in South Africa, particularly in the cities, with crime. A friend of mine had a very bad experience only last year. In front of his house there is a security officer who doesn't let anybody who is not invited in. Last year criminals waited for his neighbour, in front of this house and then followed him and stole his money and his watch. This obviously comes from the very, very big gap between poor people and rich people. Many people live in townships, in little huts with tin roofs, they don't have proper sewage or water, this is a very big problem to people's general health here in this country. HIV is another very big problem in South Africa, we have still yet to find a solution, and one of the problems is that this issue, which is a health issue and is killing people, is often mixed up in other issues that are religious or political. I hope we can find a solution to this problem soon. Although we no longer live in apartheid, the gaps and the respect between black and white people is still a problem. I hope that one day we will find ways of communicating where we truly will be equal and will be able to look at each other directly in the eye without any feelings of hatred.

Tin-Mi Hello, my name is Tin-Mi, I come from Hong Kong. I can't really remember what Hong Kong was like when it belonged to Great Britain, but my parents said it wasn't too bad. My family are Protestants, that means that we were quite a small minority in Hong Kong, there are very many people in Hong Kong with many different religions, and Protestant is, well, there's not very many of us. Err, there are lots of tourists in Hong Kong, it's very much a city for business, so sometimes there can be lots of traffic jams and the roads are blocked for much of the day. Oh, when I was younger I used to sell flowers to the tourists. I used to pick them myself and then sell them, so I guess Hong Kong is very good for business even for children. As I grew up in Hong Kong, I grew up speaking English and Chinese and so it wasn't any problem for me to speak to tourists and, and sell my flowers. Sometimes I, I used to like to go on the Asian Walk of Fame, this is because I, I really like kung-fu films and I used to like to see the name of Jackie Chan on the star. That was really cool. At the weekends I used to go to some shows. Oh and we have Disneyland, I went there sometimes with my parents. And also in Hong Kong you can go for a walk along the coastline. This is actually quite nice because you have all the buildings on one side and then the water on the other, it's quite a nice thing to do. There's, um, a place in Hong Kong called Victoria Peak, and I, I used to go there with my boyfriend, it's a really nice view of, of the whole city and the water and when the lights come on from the buildings, it's really nice, nice to see. In, um, Hong Kong you can buy lots of cheap electronic goods and, um, you might know they sell lots of fake products of brand names, but, um, actually in Hong Kong you can get the best fake products, you can almost not tell the difference, I think Hong Kong is a really cool place to go.

Ranjid Hello, as you know my name is Ranjid, and I come from Mumbai. Did you say your city is crowded? Well then you haven't been to Mumbai, because it is super crowded. Perhaps you know it by its old name, Bombay. There are almost 14 million people living on 438 km^2 of land, that's a lot of people, yeah? Most of the people are Hindu, like myself, and four languages are spoken in the city. I speak two languages, Hindi and Punjabi so communication with other people can be a problem because you might not speak their language. I am a movie fan, I love going to the cinema and watching Bollywood movies, they are my favourite. There is a great film industry in Mumbai and that is one of the reasons for the strong economy compared to other Indian cities. A lot of superstars live in Mumbai, including Shah Rukh Khan, who is my favourite. One of the bad things about Mumbai, like I mentioned earlier, is that there are too many people on too little land, and many people live in slums and are very, very poor. That is my city Mumbai, I love it and I hope you get a chance to visit it too.

Du solltest mindestens 30 Fakten nennen können. Gib dir pro Stichpunkt einen Punkt.

	Abdel	Tin-Mi	Ranjid
Place	Johannesburg (Joburg), South Africa	Hong Kong	Mumbai
General information about the city	nice place, warm and sunny, lots of tourists	people with different religions live together, lots of tourists, two languages: English and Chinese, "Asian Walk of Fame" with Asian stars like Jackie Chan	old name Bombay, almost 14 million people live on 438 km^2, most of the people are Hindu, four languages are spoken, great film industry
Positive aspects (+)	many parties at weekends, FIFA World Cup 2010	a good city for business, lots of entertainment (Disneyland, shows), walk along coastline, nice views from Victoria Peak, cheap electronics: the best fake products, really cool place	strong economy compared to other Indian cities, a lot of superstars live in Mumbai
Negative aspects (–)	crime in cities, difference between poor and rich people, townships, health problems, HIV (AIDS), blacks and whites: respect still a problem	too crowded, too much traffic, roads are blocked	super crowded, communication problem because of the different languages spoken there, too many people on too little land, slums

LANGUAGE

1 WORDS Big city life

a)

Positive aspects	Negative aspects	Places	Buildings	Transport	Verbs	Adjectives
growth magnet progress trade economy foreigners culture	poverty graffiti pollution crime homeless people waste hunger	suburb park street underground station	football stadium hotel mall skyscraper	airport tram bus taxi	attract inhabit govern trade	urban ancient modern rural financial dusty polluted

b)

1 In my city all the walls are covered with graffiti.

2 In the summer holidays, we usually take the taxi/bus/tram to the airport/park.

3 Next Saturday my favourite team is playing in our football stadium.

4 There are some ancient buildings in our city, but there are also some modern, very tall skyscrapers in the financial area where the major banks are situated.

5 When you take the bus/tram out of the city, you quickly reach a beautiful rural area.

6 One of the reasons why many cities are polluted is they don't have effective systems to deal with waste.

7 There is a lot of poverty in my city and a lot of people are homeless. They have to sleep on the streets.

8 The crime rate is high. Every day there are reports of burglaries and street shootings. As a tourist you should beware of pickpockets on the tram.

2 WORDS My city is beautiful

In my opinion, Mumbai isn't the most beautiful city in the world. There are a lot of noisy and smelly cars, which cause a lot of people sleepless nights. When the noise gets too painful, you can leave the city and relax in the endless fields which spread out around it. The movie business is a traditional and very powerful industry here and it attracts a lot of money to the city. However, there are still quite a few homeless people in the city. There are so many contrasts in Mumbai, it's the most interesting city imaginable.

3 WORDS Kung-fu fighting in Hong Kong

1 It was amazing that there were so many Chinese-speaking people at the fights.

2 At the beginning of the competition, a young, strong-looking man entered the ring.

3 His opponent was an old, well-educated man.

4 At the end, the hard-fighting champion was given a prize.

5 It may not look like it, but kung-fu is a sport for fast-moving people

6 Although it is a fight, most kung-fu fighters are peace-loving people

4 GRAMMAR Townships in Cape Town

1 Although there are rich people and nice areas in Cape Town, tourists still see a lot of people hanging around in the streets.

2 There are a lot of people living in slums.

3 In the townships you can see children playing in front of houses which are falling down.

4 On some tours tourists listen to people playing traditional music.

WRITING

Landslide hits an orphanage

Mögliche Lösungen:

a)

no direct answers to Wh-questions, lots of details, subjective opinions by the journalist and eye-witnesses, no official opinion, lots adjectives, direct speech (instead of indirect speech), exclamation marks

b)

The article is about a catastrophe in a small village near Mumbai. (3P) Six children are believed to have been killed by a landslide which fell on an orphanage. (3P) The roof collapsed while they were having dinner. (3P) Three adults, who work for the orphanage, are also missing. (2P) Officials, firefighters and Red Cross members don't believe they will be found alive. (2P) Nearby houses have been evacuated, because people are afraid there might be further landslides.

c)

Landslide hits orphanage and kills six children (1P)

A landslide hit an orphanage in a village near Mumbai today. (3P)

Although a large number of workers were involved in the rescue, they couldn't help the children buried by the landslide. (1P) Six children aged eight to ten are believed to have lost their lives in the landslide, rescue workers are still looking for their bodies. (3P) Officials say the roof couldn't carry the heavy load and collapsed, burying the children underneath it. (2P)

Three adults, who were working for the orphanage, are also missing. (2P) The search for survivors had to stop because of heavy rain. (1P)

Nearby houses had to be evacuated because officials were afraid of a further landslide tonight. (3P)

SPEAKING

08 Booking a holiday

a)

Sarah Hello, this is Sarah McLeod speaking. I'd like to book a flight, please.

TA Good afternoon, Madam. Where would you like to go?

Sarah To Bern in Switzerland, please. Leaving from Manchester.

TA OK, and when would you like to travel?

Sarah It's my grandmother's birthday on the 21st of June, so I'd like to arrive on the 19th.

TA I see. And how long do you intend to stay?

Sarah I was thinking of staying a week so I can go hiking in the mountains.

TA How nice! Let me check for available flights. Is it just you travelling?

Sarah Yes, my brother has to work.

TA I understand. OK, here we have a flight leaving Manchester on the 19th and coming back exactly one week later.

Sarah Great! And how much is it?

TA It's 250 pounds including taxes.

Sarah Gosh. I didn't know it was going to be that expensive ...

TA It's the busy season, you know, so prices are going up.

Sarah Is there no other chance of getting a cheaper ticket?

TA You could take a coach, that would definitely save you money.

Sarah No, thank you. I don't want to go by ferry or through the tunnel.

TA Then this is the only offer I have. I'm sorry. Do you want me to book it?

Sarah OK then.

TA Do you want me to book accommodation for you, too?

Sarah No, thank you. I'm going to stay at my granny's.

TA I see. That's nice. For the flight I need your full name again, please, and your address.

Sarah OK, that's Sarah McLeod, 32 Hillborough Street, Didsbury, Manchester BE7 643 ...

09 Now you

b)

Language school	UG Language school, you're talking to Susan Hiller. How can I help you?
You	Hello, this is ... speaking. I'd like to book a language holiday, please. (1P)
Language school	Good afternoon. Where would you like to go?
You	I'd like to go to Brighton, please. So I can relax on the beach and learn English. (2P)
Language school	OK, and when would you like to travel?
You	I thought of going there in the summer holidays, starting on the 21st of June. (1P)
Language school	And how long do you intend to stay?
You	I was thinking of staying there for two weeks. And I'd like to take the train and stay in a bed & breakfast. (3P)
Language school	I understand. OK, here we have an offer for a language holiday. It's £500 per week for the course and the train ticket if you stay in a bed & breakfast.
You	Gosh. I didn't know it was going to be that expensive. £500 is quite a lot of money. (1P)
Language school	It's the busy season, you know, so prices are going up.
You	Is there no other way of getting there cheaper? (1P)
Language school	You could stay in a host family instead of the bed and breakfast, that would definitely save you some money. It would be £800 for two weeks. Would that be within your budget?
You	Yes, that's my limit. I can't pay more than that and I really want to stay for two weeks. (2P)
Language school	I see. You'll have such a brilliant time in Brighton! I now need your full name again, please and your address.
You	OK, that's ... (1P)

READING

a)

Mögliche Lösungen:

1 In the text, teachers are described as 'education distributors', so parents can be seen as 'education consumers'.

2 More and more students are acting aggressively at school. They slam doors, throw fire crackers and tear pictures from the walls.

3 In some families the children are the only ones who have to get up in the mornings.

4 Students do not only beat each other up, they also use trash cans as footballs.

5 It is important that parents understand the school's concept and know what their rights and responsibilities are.

6 If children were cars, parents would ask for the best treatment possible.

7 Parents' relationship to their car mechanic is often closer than the relationship to their children's teachers.

8 The fact that parents need advice about the education of their offspring is shown by the great success of TV shows like 'Super nanny'.

9 It would be much easier if parents and teachers worked together and trusted each other more.

10 In order to achieve this both sides have to overcome their prejudices.

b)

The article deals with violence in schools in big cities and the role which parents can play in finding solutions. (2P) Students are often violent towards other students and they also damage school property. (2P) In rural areas problems of this kind are unheard of. (1P) One solution to this problem is to get parents and schools working together to support children's education. (2P) This is often difficult to achieve because many parents do not know how to help and need professional advice. (2P) This can be seen in the success of TV shows and magazines that deal with educating children. (1P)

c)

There are people who say that parents should be more involved in their children's school life. (1P)
On the one hand, I think it is important for parents to be involved in what their children learn and how they do at school. (2P) My mother, for example, asks me every afternoon when I come home how school was, and I tell her about my day. (2P) Sometimes I do not want to talk, and that's OK too. (2P)
On the other hand, I would not like her to come to school every week and get on my teachers' nerves! (2P)
All in all, I think it is good if parents take an interest in their children's school life, but they should not know everything and be there all the time. (2P)

LANGUAGE

1 WORDS A crossword

Across

1 commuter 3 travel guide 5 ceiling 7 concrete 9 occupy 11 squatter 13 scent

Down

2 fan 4 underwear 6 cell 8 horizon 10 columns 12 beggar

2 GRAMMAR Bollywood

1 People in Mumbai, working many hours a day, like light entertainment.
2 Many people, wishing to spend time with their families, often watch Bollywood films on TV.
3 Women watching these movies love the romantic stories, and often have a box of handkerchiefs on their knees.
4 Even in the early days of Bollywood, characters sang in the street and were accompanied by big dancing groups.
5 At the end, the hero, winning the girl he loves, kisses her as the crowd dances in the background.

Lerntipp **Besonderheiten bei der Schreibung**

Infinitive	Present participle	Past participle
plan	planning	planned
dance	dancing	danced
try	trying	tried

Lerne die past participle-Formen der unregelmäßigen Verben in der „dritten Spalte" auf S. 240–241 in deinem Englischbuch auswendig.

3 GRAMMAR Meeting a Bollywood star

1 Walking through the busy streets of Mumbai, I looked into a café at the corner.
2 (After) having walked through the crowded café, I found an empty table in a corner.
3 (After) having ordered a hot chocolate, my favourite star asked me if he could sit at my table.
4 Having just seen his latest movie at the cinema, I asked him all about how it was made.
5 (After) having met him, I went home not being able to think about anything else any more.
6 (While) having dinner, I thought about the afternoon at the café.
7 The next day I saw my favourite star on TV giving an interview while teaching a dancing class.

MEDIATION

The forbidden parts of New York City

Es handelt sich um eine Tour durch das nächtliche New York. (1P)

Man fährt mit der U-Bahn zum Central Park und geht dort nachts spazieren. Vom abgelegenen Hügel hat man einen fabelhaften Blick auf die Skyline von Manhattan. Dann geht's weiter mit der U-Bahn in die berüchtigte Bronx, wo man eine Gang treffen und seine Hände an einem brennenden Faß wärmen kann. (3P)

Zu beachten ist, dass Personen mit Herzkrankheiten, Herzschrittmachern oder Bluthochdruck nicht teilnehmen sollten. Wertsachen über 100 $ sollten im Hotel gelassen, und Schmuck und Uhren möglichst nicht getragen werden. (4P)

Die Tour kostet 10 $, ermäßigt 5 $ für Minderjährige, Studenten und Senioren. (2P)

LISTENING

10 How social is the social network?

Brian Sarah, do you know what's going on with this webpage?

Sarah I dunno, but, erm, hang on let me see …

Brian Is it the right webpage that we need for the information?

Sarah I don't think so, oh I don't give a … can we just quickly, can I just check my Facebook because there is some important information for that party on Saturday?

Brian We shouldn't be doing Facebook, we should be working on this …

Sarah Oh I know, oh goody goody two-shoes.

Brian No, no, that's just not right, come on, let's, let's get back … erm, wait a minute I think that's Mr Fitzgerald.

Mr Fitzgerald Where did I find that information again? Goddamn I put it somewhere, I just can't …

Sarah Oh, here we go … hello Mr Fitzgerald.

Brian Hello Mr Fitzgerald.

Mr Fitzgerald Ah, hello, hi, hi, how's things? OK?

Brian Very good, we're working really hard for our new project.

Mr Fitzgerald Hmm, so what are you doing then?

Sarah Research.

Mr Fitzgerald Research? Research into what?

Sarah Stuff.

Mr Fitzgerald Stuff, what sort of stuff? And you're doing it on the internet are you, with the computers?

Sarah Yes, it's for the assignment on Friday.

Mr Fitzgerald Oh, so what's this then, a chat room or something, or, one of these social networking sites?

Brian Oh, well, we were just taking five minutes.

Sarah Yeah, that was just recreational.

Mr Fitzgerald Oh, so oh don't worry I don't know very much about them, what, social networking sites or something they call them, don't they?

Sarah It's called Facebook, you might have heard of it.

Mr Fitzgerald Facebook?

Sarah Yeah.

Mr Fitzgerald Something to do with faces?

Brian No, that's …

Mr Fitzgerald Do you put your face on there?

Brian It's not exactly like that, it's about, err, it's a social network site. It's where people meet people and keep up with other people's information.

Sarah It's really cool.

Mr Fitzgerald	Hmm, information, it sounds, hmm, well, very interesting, I mean I'm not against the new media, or anything like that, I must admit I've got a few doubts about it but, err, I suppose I can see its advantages. Obviously it's easier to communicate with people – you can communicate with them all over the world, can't you?
Sarah	Exactly, that's why I'm using it, I'm sort of just keeping in touch with my friends that I can't see every day, you know?
Brian	Yeah in, in my opinion it's good but there are some bad things there.
Mr Fitzgerald	Right …
Sarah	Oh, like what?
Mr Fitzgerald	Like what?
Brian	Well I heard a story about … there are certain employers who browse through social network sites to find out more information about people who work for them, or applicants who are going to work for them.
Sarah	Yeah, what's so bad about that? Sorry, but I don't understand what you mean.
Brian	Well, it's, it's people checking up on you and also other things that I've read about are things like where people have been molested.
Mr Fitzgerald	Well, this is what I was going to say, there are dangers and I think young people especially should be made aware of them.
Brian	Yeah, that's a good point.
Mr Fitzgerald	You give away so much information about yourself, to whom? I mean to complete strangers, people that you know nothing about …
Sarah	I see what you mean, but if you stay in your network, you've got your friends and only they can access your information, you know I'm very proud of having 150 online friends, you know. I get to know more people all the time. In fact, I think, you know it's very possible that I will find a boyfriend there, one day.
Brian	Oh God.
Sarah	Well, Brian yes I know but …
Brian	That's a good point, Sarah.
Mr Fitzgerald	But I mean you put sort of, you know, you don't allow embarrassing party pictures or anything like that to be, err, … … and the other thing about that, I mean once a photograph's taken, it's taken and it could pop up on the internet in years' time, I mean it could be seen by, you know, who knows by whom …
Brian	Oh that's a good point …
Mr Fitzgerald	… In twenty, thirty years' time when you're married with three kids or even a grandmother or grandfather and these photographs of you running stark naked around at the parties suddenly appear and …
Sarah	Yeah, I agree with you but … well if you did it, you did it, right, why should we be ashamed about it?
Brian	Oh you've seen her homepage then?
Sarah	What? Shut up!
Mr Fitzgerald	Well, do you want the rest of the world to see that in twenty, thirty years' time? And another thing, while we're on the subject of all of this computer stuff, and, err, networking sites and so on, I would … I must admit, I am a little bit old-fashioned, but I do believe in the good old-fashioned book and I'd like to see students reading books a little bit more …

Sarah	That's a totally different thing.
Mr Fitzgerald	Rather than spending all their time on computer screens and …
Brian	I see what you mean.
Mr Fitzgerald	Jumping from one thing to another, at least with a book you go by page to page and you get a chance to, sort of, actually get into the subject and it's …
Brian	That's a good point.
Sarah	You can't talk to people on a book though.
Mr Fitzgerald	It's not as trivial as a lot of this information seems to be that we get on, on the internet. That, that's my point.
Sarah	Yeah, OK.
Brian	Yeah, well I only use the internet from time to time, so this doesn't really happen to me, and I only chat to people that I know, for example, if you don't know the person, it could be anyone, and it could be quite dangerous.
Mr Fitzgerald	This is my point.
Sarah	Yeah, but I spend three hours a day chatting, yeah, and I stay …
Brian	At least.
Sarah	Well, quite, OK, and checking my other social network accounts, but you know I move, on the internet I move within a very limited space, you know … I chat to my friends, I don't always invite new people to watch my, view my pictures.
Brian	Yes, but sometimes you don't know who the other person is and …
Sarah	Of course because they have to log in.
Brian	Yeah, but they might be a friend of a friend of a friend and you might accept.
Sarah	Yes that's true, I mean 150 online friends, that's …
Brian	You've got 150 friends?
Sarah	Yes I do [sic; besser wäre *have*].
Brian	And you know them all?
Sarah	Yes I do.
Brian	By name?
Sarah	Yes I do.
Brian	And face?
Sarah	Well, yes, some of them are friends of friends and some of them are people I want to meet one day.
Brian	And some of them are people that you met randomly once on a bus …
Sarah	Yes, so what?
Brian	Well they're not really friends then are they?
Sarah	They were hot!
Brian	Good point, I do agree with you. That's a very good point.
Sarah	Thank you. (…)

1 Who said what?

a)

Mr Fitzgerald: 1, 4, 8

Sarah: 5, 9, 11, 12

Brian: 2, 6, 13

Ohne Zuordnung: 3, 7, 10

b)

1 sitting at a computer, internet research

2 concentrate on research for a project

3 people meet other people + keep in touch with them

4 has doubts about them

5 some good + some bad things

6 people give away too much information about themselves

7 150

8 a boyfriend

9 you can get more deeply into the subject

10 about 3 hours

2 Discussing social networking sites

a) / b)

Mögliche Lösungen:

Pros (+)	Cons (–)
– Easy to communicate with people all over the world. – Keep in touch with friends you can't see every day. – Get to know more people all the time. – (See what old friends look like today.)	– Employers browse through social networking sites to find information about job applicants. – (Embarrassing party) photographs can pop up on the internet even years later. – If you don't know the person you are chatting to, it could be dangerous. – (It takes a lot of time.)

c)

Many people say that using social networking sites is dangerous. (1P)

On the one hand, I think that using Facebook and other similar sites is fun. It's such an easy way to communicate with my friends. Since I've put my profile online, I feel I know a lot more about my real friends, and I've got in touch with some of my friends from kindergarten too. (4P)

On the other hand, I spend about an hour a day at least online. Sometimes I think this is too much time. I would rather meet my real friends instead. (3P)

LANGUAGE

1 WORDS You're beautiful, it's true

1 Your grandmother always told us what a handsome man your grandfather was when he was young.

2 Oh, such a pretty baby! How old is she?

3 I think you're the most beautiful woman I've ever met.

4 Corsica is a lovely/beautiful place to visit in spring.

5 Jim's good-looking, but he knows it and, if you ask me, that doesn't make him so attractive.

2 WORDS Looking for Mr Right

Hi there,

My name is Sarah and I'm talking to all those good-looking/handsome boys out there! I don't like questionnaires, so I'm going to express my thoughts and tell you a bit about myself in a short text. I'm sixteen and still go to school. In my free time I do some social work. I help old people with their shopping. I don't mind being single because I've got really great friends, but secretly I'm looking for a relationship. Only write to me if you're serious and looking for a girlfriend. I don't want a boyfriend who will cheat on me or chuck me after a few weeks! If you think you might be interested, then ask me out on a date – as a tip I love pizza. Looking forward to your reply.

Love,

Sarah

3 GRAMMAR What will the future bring?

"Will we stay together when we leave school?" is a question which young people in relationships often ask themselves. You might have spoken to your boyfriend or girlfriend about what you are going to do after school and it's an important conversation to have. Perhaps you are going to attend / will attend the same university, perhaps you are going (to go) / will go to different universities, or one of you is going to stay / will stay at home whilst the other goes away. Whatever happens, your relationship probably won't be the same as it is now. There are all sorts of questions to answer. How often are you going to see one another? Are you going to live together?

These are things which I've been thinking about a lot. Next Monday I am meeting my girlfriend, and we are going to discuss these ideas. I wonder what she will say. Luckily there's still some time left before we have to make up our minds.

4 GRAMMAR Simple present for the future

1 Josh – does the film start at 7.30 or 8 o'clock this evening?

2 The Scout soup kitchen opens for the first time this Tuesday.

3 I finish work at 5.30 on Wednesday, so I should be home by 6.

4 The bus leaves at 6.30, so I've got plenty of time to get to work.

5 What time does the train get to Cologne?

WRITING

Social networking sites – an essay

The two faces of Facebook

Facebook is an online social networking site with millions of users worldwide. It was invented in 2004 by Mark Zuckerberg, today the youngest billionaire in the world. Facebook users create a personal profile, add other users as friends and exchange messages. Your profile can include photos, lists of personal interests, contact details, and other personal information. Every user must register before using the site. You must be at least 13 years old to register.

I really like the platform because it makes it so easy to keep in touch with your friends and get to know new people. At the moment, I have 200 friends on my list – friends, their friends and their friends' friends.

Of course I do not know all of them personally, but it is fun to have a look at their profiles and to know what other people are doing. When I am on holiday, for example, I usually post some pictures of myself lying on the beach, just to make people at home feel a little bit jealous.

However, although I think Facebook is a very positive thing, I know that there are some dangers. I realize that not all my online friends are real friends, and I do not post party pictures or photos where I am in embarrassing situations.

All in all, I deal with my online profile very carefully and so I can see no reason not to use this entertaining platform.

Bewertung und Punkte bei Schreibaufgaben

Dein Text enthält ...	**Punkte**
1. Einleitung: Einführung ins Thema	7
2. Deine Thesen und Argumente für oder gegen die Fragestellung	7
3. Thesen und Argumente der Gegenseite	3
4. Schlussfolgerung: deine Meinung nach Zusammenfassung	3
	20

SPEAKING

11 Would you like to go out with me?

Luca Hi, I'm Luca, I'm new in your class.

Peter Oh, yes, I know. I'm Peter.

Luca Hi, I think you're a really nice class.

Peter Oh thanks!

Luca Where I come from we like to play tricks on our teachers.

Peter All right.

Luca What's the funniest trick that you or, or anyone else has played on your teacher?

Peter Um, well actually I haven't ever really played a trick on my teacher, but a couple of weeks ago someone in the class did, yeah they put, um, glue on the teacher's chair, and then she sat on it!

Luca Oh gosh that would have been really funny!

Peter It was!

Luca What should I know about the school?

Peter We have a really strong music department, so at the end of the year our musicals are really, really good, and it's the same with the drama group, they're really, really good. And also there's the school party next week, don't miss that. It's a lot of fun, it's always a really great night.

Luca Oh, OK, right, thanks! We've just moved here from London, so I have no idea what there is to do around here, um, can you give me some suggestions, or …

Peter Err, yeah, yeah, I mean, do you have any plans for the weekend?

Luca No …

Peter There's, there's, err, the local cinema here is really, really great, they play really cool movies, and, um, my friends and I are going, maybe you'd like to come too, I mean with my friends?

Luca Yeah, that, that would be great.

Peter Yeah? All right.

Luca Oh thanks. Oh, this is my stop – I have to get off. But, I'll see you tomorrow!

Peter Yes! Great, um, yeah, looking forward to it!

Luca Bye!

Peter Bye!

12, 13 Now you: Asking a girl/boy out

Mögliche Lösungen:

Girl/Boy Hi, my name is Luca/Luke. I'm new in your class.

You I'm Sascha. Nice to meet you. (1P)

Girl/Boy What's the funniest trick you or your classmates have ever played on your teachers?

You Oh, I don't know really, let me think. Last week we put a bucket of water on the door, which fell down when the teacher entered the classroom. Yeah, that was a classic. You would have loved it! (4P)

Girl/Boy What should I know about the school?

You Well, there are some really good activities. You should join one of the sports clubs. Basketball is great. Our teachers are alright, but beware of Mr Löwe. You don't want him as an enemy ... (4P)

Girl/Boy Ah, I see. We have just moved here from London, and I don't really know what there is to do round here. Any suggestions?

You Oh yes, there's quite a lot to do here. How about the youth centre? It's really cool. Don't miss that. It's always a lot of fun. You can play pool or table tennis there or just chill out and listen to music. Do you have any plans for tomorrow? If you like, I can introduce you to the people there. Maybe you'd like to come? (6P)

Girl/Boy Oh, that would be great. Oh, this is my stop, I have to get off here. But see you tomorrow!

You Yes! I'm looking forward to it! We'll have a really great time. Bye! (2P)

READING

Bono: a celebrity campaigner

1 Missing headings

A5, B4, C2, D1, E3

2 About the text

a)

Mögliche Lösungen:

Amnesty international tour of the US, Band Aid, Live Aid concerts, visit to Ethiopia, songs with political messages, contact with politicians, helped to create the organizations DATA, EDUN and ONE

b)

In 1979 the Secret Policeman's Ball got Bono interested in charity work. He started getting involved in charity concerts including the Amnesty International tour of America and Live Aid. In 1985 Bono and his wife spent time working in an orphanage in Ethiopia. After this experience, Bono decided that he would do what he could to fight poverty.

LANGUAGE

1 WORDS A network

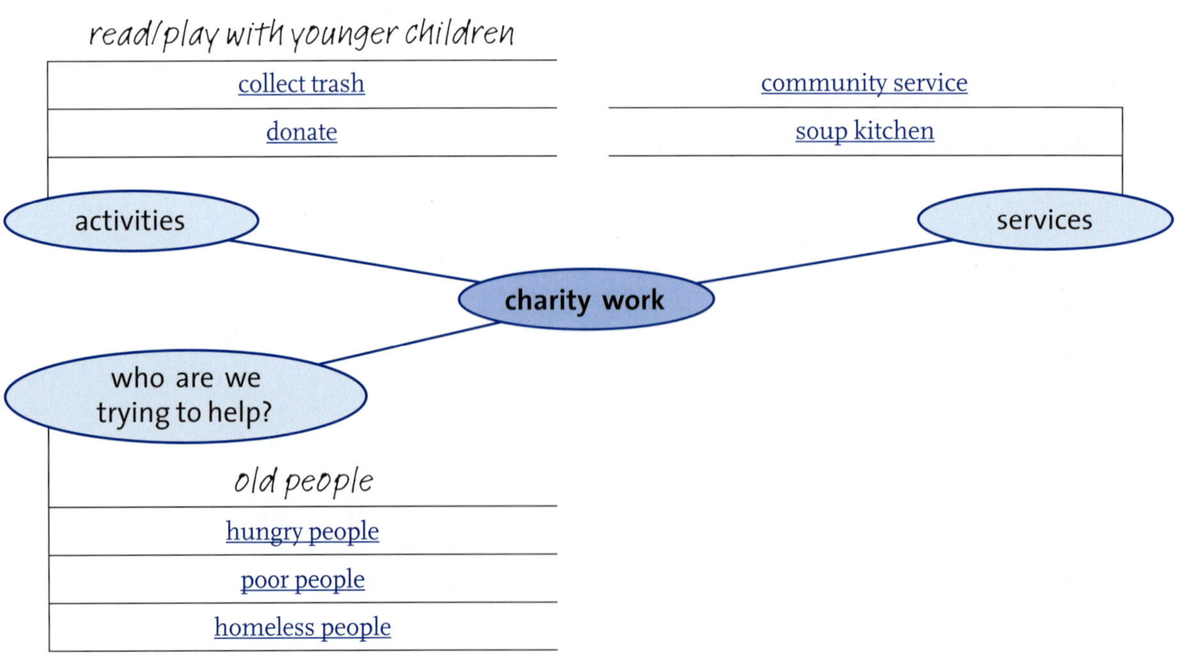

b)

With the Scouts we regularly do community service. One of the things we do every week is collect trash. The last time we went out we found an old fridge which someone had just left in the woods. And guess what, it still worked! So we cleaned it up and sold it at a flea market. We decided to donate the money we got to the local soup kitchen which provides poor and homeless people with a warm meal, so that they don't go hungry.

2 WORDS Using new words

1 I was playing with my mobile phone as I was walking down the street and I bumped into a lamppost. How embarrassing!

2 Laura does a paper round. She delivers newspapers to the people in my street.

3 Peter likes animals. Yesterday I saw him walking his neighbour's dog.

4 David's such a gentleman. He's so polite and always thinks of other people.

5 Gosh, there is a long queue. We'll have to be patient.

6 Don't pretend to like mathematics. I know you hate it!

7 I don't go out after dark. I'm afraid of ghosts.

3 GRAMMAR An incredible trip

1 They made us clean our room ourselves once a week.

2 They let us stay out until 2 in the morning.

3 They let us use their private TV and PC any time.

4 They made us / let us eat fish or meat every day.

5 They made us pay €50 extra for day trips.

6 They made us look after their baby José for an hour every day.

4 GRAMMAR The Scout hut

1 They cleaned the Scout hut themselves.

2 But they had the windows cleaned by window cleaners.

3 Josh cut the grass in front of the Scout hut himself.

4 They had the walls painted by a painter.

5 Josh built a chair himself.

6 But they had the roof repaired by professionals.

MEDIATION

Doing community service

Dear Ahmed, (1P)

The text is about the possibility of spending a year doing volunteer work. (1P)

It says there are opportunities to work with children or young people, with disabled people, in hospitals, old people's homes, in sports clubs or cultural institutions. (6P)

The programme is for people aged between 16 and 27. (1P)

You don't have to stay in Germany/Hesse to do the volunteer work – the FSJ also offers jobs in foreign countries. (1P)

It's a good way to use the time between school and starting a career. (1P)

As a volunteer you get pocket money, food and accommodation. (1P)

You can find out more information on the website www.fsj-hessen.de. There you can also find information about the organizations that offer volunteer placements. (2P) There are also descriptions of the kinds of jobs on offer that might make it easier to decide what kind of placement you want to do and where you want to do it. (2P)

I hope that helps you understand the website. (1P)

Best wishes, (1P)

Paul

A5

English G 21

Klassenarbeitstrainer

für Schülerinnen und Schüler

mit Lösungen
Lerntipps

Cornelsen

English G 21 • Band A 5

Klassenarbeitstrainer mit Lösungen und Lerntipps

Konzeption
Dr. Ursula Mulla und Nogi Mulla, Germering

Erarbeitet von
Martin Kohn, Frankfurt/Main
Bärbel Schweitzer, M.A., Staufen

In Zusammenarbeit mit der Englischredaktion
Dr. Christiane Kallenbach (Projektleitung)
Gwendolyn Düwel (verantwortliche Redakteurin), Ulrike Berendt
Susanne Bennetreu, Stefanie Juhnke (Bildredaktion)

Beratende Mitwirkung
Katrin Häntzschel, Wiesa

Tonaufnahmen
Clarity Studio Berlin

Illustrationen
Anne-Claire Martin, Berlin (S. 57); Constanze Schargan, Berlin (S. 6; 9; 10; 19)

Bildquellen
Alamy, Abingdon (S. 8: Oredia; S. 16: Daniel Templeton; S. 18: Alan King engraving; S. 26: mediablitzimages (uk) Limited; S. 31: Yadid Levy; S. 36: Yan Liao (RF); S. 37: Ulrich Doering; S. 40: Angela Hampton Picture; S. 53: AlamyCelebrity); **Alice Springs School of the Air**, 80 Head Street, Alice Springs Northern Territory Australien, www.assoa.nt.edu.au (S. 14); **Corbis**, Düsseldorf (S. 4 Mitte: Reuters / Darren Staples; S. 38: Demotix / JOE MWANGI; S. 52 oben: Hans Neleman; S. 56: Ocean (RF)); **Getty Images**, München (S. 13: Sindre Ellingsen; S. 43: DreamPictures); **iStockphoto**, Calgary (S. 4 re.: Sara Winter, 2. v. li.: David Freund; S. 11: twobluedogs; S. 21: sturti; S. 24: londoneye; S. 33: tunart; S. 46 li.: David Sucsy, re.: oneclearvision; S. 50: 101dalmatians; S. 52 unten re.: drbimages); **Moritz Schweitzer**, Villingen-Schwenningen (S. 5); **Shutterstock**, New York (S. 4 li.: Taras Vyshnya, 2. v. re.: markrhiggins; S. 7 li.: Paul Coartney, re.: John Carnemolla; S. 23: stefanolunardi; S. 27: Minerva Studio; S. 29: Tracy Whiteside; S. 34 li.: tan4ikk, Mitte: szefei, re.: PT Images; S. 39: Elena Elisseeva; S. 46 Mitte: Goodluz; S. 49: Goodluz; S. 52 unten li.: Nejron Photo; S. 55: Monkey Business Images)

Textquellen
S. 14: Alice Springs School of the Air. From Alice Springs School of the Air, 80 Head Street, Alice Springs Northern Territory Australien, www.assoa.nt.edu.au; S. 58: FSJ in Hessen. From *Freiwilliges Soziales Jahr in Hessen*. http://www.fsj-hessen.de/global/show_document.asp?id=aaaaaaaaaaadmrj. Hessisches Sozialministerium

Titelbild
Alamy, Abingdon (Henry Westheim Photography); **Corel Library** (flag Hintergund (M))

Layout und technische Umsetzung
Heike Freund, Hameln

Umschlaggestaltung
Klein und Halm Grafikdesign, Berlin

www.cornelsen.de
www.EnglishG.de

1. Auflage, 3. Druck 2015

Druck: H. Heenemann, Berlin

ISBN 978-3-06-032324-1

PEFC zertifiziert
Dieses Produkt stammt aus nachhaltig bewirtschafteten Wäldern und kontrollierten Quellen.
www.pefc.de

INHALT

Schon wieder eine Klassenarbeit ...

Liebe Schülerin, lieber Schüler,
wer sich gut vorbereitet, kann der nächsten Klassenarbeit gelassen entgegenblicken. Der Klassenarbeitstrainer unterstützt dich ganz gezielt beim Üben für alle Klassenarbeiten. Du findest zu jeder Unit zwei Klassenarbeiten, mit denen du alle Fertigkeiten (skills) trainieren kannst, die du für die Klassenarbeiten benötigst.

Einige Tipps für ein erfolgreiches Lernen mit deinem Klassenarbeitstrainer:

Vorbereitung
Informiere dich genau über die Inhalte der kommenden Klassenarbeit. In einem Lernplan legst du fest, welche Aufgaben du an welchem Tag bearbeiten willst. Plane dazu genügend Zeit ein. Bei Unklarheiten solltest du zuerst im Englischbuch nachsehen. Erst wenn du hier nicht weiter kommst, holst du dir Hilfe von anderen. Am Tag vor der Arbeit wiederholst du nur kurz.

Inhaltsverzeichnis
Im Inhaltsverzeichnis kannst du ablesen, welche Kompetenzen pro Klassenarbeit geübt werden. Oft gibt es auch zwei unterschiedliche Aufgaben zu einer Kompetenz, z.B. zum Listening oder zum Writing. Wähle eine aus oder löse beide Aufgaben.

Lernheft
Führe ein Heft für Schreibaufgaben und zusätzliche Übungen. Achte auf Übersichtlichkeit (Datum, Überschrift, Aufgabe, Seite). Lege auf der ersten Seite ein Inhaltsverzeichnis an. So kannst du bei Unklarheiten immer wieder nachschlagen. Es hilft dir auch, wenn du eine Aufgabe wiederholen möchtest.

Lösungsheft
Vergleiche deine Lösungen mit den möglichen Lösungen. Sieh dir dabei deine Fehler ganz genau an und analysiere sie. Nur so kannst du aus deinen Fehlern lernen. Im Lösungsheft findest du Lerntipps mit weiteren Übungen und auch die Hörtexte.

Punkteschlüssel
Bei jeder Klassenarbeit ist die Gesamtpunktzahl für alle Aufgaben angegeben. Solltest du beim Lernen eigene Schwerpunkte setzen und deswegen Aufgaben weglassen, musst du die Gesamtpunktzahl neu ermitteln. Mit dem Punkteschlüssel kannst du deine Leistung einschätzen.

Übrigens: Die Klassenarbeiten in diesem Heft prüfen das Gelernte sehr ausführlich ab.
Du brauchst daher für die Bearbeitung länger als eine Schulstunde.

Jetzt kann es aber wirklich losgehen – **let's get started!**

All the best,

Bärbel Schweitzer und Martin Kohn

Gesamtpunktzahl ohne Speaking	_____ /85	Note _____
Gesamtpunktzahl mit Speaking	_____ /101	Note _____

LISTENING

_____ /19

01 **1 A high school photo competition** _____ /9

a) *Look at the photos, then listen to the discussion and write the correct number in the boxes. Explain your choice. (6P)*

☞ Falls du die Namen nicht gleich zuordnen kannst, mache dir Notizen dazu, was die Jury-Mitglieder über die Fotos sagen.

A

B

C

D

E

F

b) *Which picture would you give a prize to? Give reasons for your answer. (Three sentences) (3P)*

02 2 An interview for the school radio station

____/ 10

a) *Listen to the radio interview and put the information about Maya in the correct order. (5P)*

	She was very excited when the art teacher announced her name.
	She started taking pictures ten years ago.
	She has already participated in a photo competition.
	Her best photographs show her family and friends.
	She thinks the light was very good.

b) *Listen again carefully. Then read the following sentences. Some of them are true, some of them are false. Tick the box and correct the false statements. (5P)*

Sentence	True	False	Correction
Maya started taking photos when she was five.			
She wasn't successful in her first competition.			
Maya planned to take a picture of her favourite kids' playground.			
Maya likes touristy photos very much.			
The prize is a very good camera.			

MEDIATION

___/9

A photo competition

The following text is taken from the Australian magazine 'The one and only Australia' which has started a photo competition.

'The one and only Australia' monthly photo competition

We love everything that's special, wonderful and unusual about Australia.
And we love seeing what you like about our country too. This month the topic of our photo competition is:

One moment in Sydney

Enter our competition and you could win a $500 camera!

How to enter:
When you've chosen your photo, write a short description of it.
You should also give details of when and where the photo was taken.

Some rules:
The closing date for your entries is October 10 at midnight.
The competition is open to anybody aged 16 and over.
You should send your name, your full address and telephone number and a caption.
Photos must be at least 1 MB in size.
Each person is allowed to hand in one photo only. Of course you can take part again next month!

E-mail your photo to:
photocompetition@theoneandonlyaustralia.au
Please note that letters (with photos) sent by post will not be accepted in the competition.

The winner:
The winner's photo will be published in our magazine next month together with his or her name.

Think you've got a winning photo? We're waiting to see it!

Einer deiner Freunde ist ein guter Fotograf und möchte an diesem Wettbewerb teilnehmen. Hilf ihm, den Text zu verstehen. Schreibe deine Lösung in dein Lernheft.

Teile ihm mit ...
1. was man alles einsenden muss
2. die Regeln *(mind. vier)*
3. den Preis
4. wann ein Foto nicht zum Wettbewerb zugelassen wird
5. was geschieht, wenn man mit einem Foto gewonnen hat *(zwei Dinge)*

LANGUAGE

____ /27

1 WORDS Melanie reports from Australia

____ /8

Melanie from Osnabrück is spending a year in Australia living with a family on a farm. Once a week she writes a letter to her class in Germany, in English, of course!

Help Melanie by completing the text with words from the box. Be careful: there are three more words than you need.

atmosphere • Aussies • barbecue • cancer • careful • climate • dirt • emus • gorgeous • instructor • mate • outback • ozone • reef • serious • sunscreen • ultraviolet • unique • wetsuit

On the farm I met Joey, the 16-year-old son of the family. When I first saw him, I thought he was ____________________. I thought that he would be very ____________________ because he was showing me my work on the farm, but in fact he spent all his time laughing and making jokes. To start with I couldn't help laughing with him, but because he was my ____________________, I became nervous and began to freak out.

One day he told me about his favourite hobby: he and his ____________________ like riding their dirt bikes on ____________________ roads through the Australian ____________________. Sometimes they see animals like ____________________ and koalas. That's quite impressive, isn't it? Because the ____________________ in Australia is so hot and sunny, Joey and his friend have to put on ____________________ before they go out even when they're wearing special clothes. The hole in the ____________________ layer lets dangerous ____________________ rays pass into the atmosphere. Even if you're sitting in the shade, you have to be ____________________ because the sun is still dangerous. It's a really serious problem and a lot of Australians do develop skin ____________________.

After they go for their bike rides, Joey and his mate like to go for a ____________________ down at the beach and they invite other friends too. The ____________________ even have beach parties on Christmas Day! That must be a really ____________________ experience!

2 Tricky translations

____/10

Melanie was surprised when Joey asked her out to an Australian restaurant one evening. Read what happened and fill in the correct translation of the German words.

Last Friday was the ____________________ (groß) day: our date! We met ____________________ (vor) the farmhouse. I ____________________ (tragen) my best dress and Joey looked great. He offered to ____________________ (tragen) my jacket for me – that was very sweet! Joey wanted to ____________________ (fahren) to the restaurant but the car was broken so we had to wait for another hour and then ____________________ (fahren) by bus. He ____________________ (machen) a short call and asked his mate if he could help him repair the car the next day. ____________________ (während) we were waiting for the bus, we laughed a lot. That was a good start! When we arrived at the restaurant, we took our seats and the waiter ____________________ (bringen) the menu. It was very difficult to choose because everything sounded great. It ____________________ (brauchen) us ages to decide and I ____________________ (brauchen) Joey to help me, but we finally ordered. We talked a lot ____________________ (während) dinner and Joey was so funny. I have to say that when I first met him, I didn't really like him. He laughed at me because I didn't know how to ride a horse. And then, just three days ____________________ (vor), I got very angry with him because he was acting like my ____________________ (groß) brother and correcting me all the time. But ____________________ (während) our date he was lovely.

It was the chef himself who ____________________ (bringen) us our dinner! It was fantastic.

When the waiter had ____________________ (bringen) the plates away and we had finished our drinks, we decided to ____________________ (machen) something else. I thought we should go to the cinema, and Joey agreed. The film was very scary and I was happy that Joey was with me because he's very ____________________ (groß) so I wasn't afraid in the dark streets after the film. When we got home, he kissed me good night. It was a fantastic date and I hope we'll ____________________ (machen) it again very soon!

3 GRAMMAR Melanie's time in Australia

____/9

Today is September 1st. Take a look at the pictures to find out what Melanie and Joey did over the past year, what they usually do and what they are doing now in Australia. Use either ***simple present, present progressive, simple past*** *or* ***past perfect****. Write one sentence for each picture using the correct tense.*

Die Verwendung der Zeiten
Sieh dir die Tabelle mit den Signalwörtern an, bevor du die Aufgabe löst. Sie helfen dir dabei, die richtige Zeitform zu wählen. Achte beim Lösen auf die Vorzeitigkeit.

Tense	Signal Words
Simple Present	usually, every day, once a week, every year, always, often, never
Present Progressive	now, at the moment
Simple Past	yesterday, last (week, month, year, Friday ...)
Past Perfect	before, after

MEDIATION

____/10

Welcome to Queensland!

You are planning a holiday in Australia with your parents. You found the following text on the internet.

Welcome to Queensland!

You like the sun?
You want to enjoy 300 warm and sunny days a year?
Then you should visit Queensland – where everyone is happy!

Queensland has so much to offer, it will be hard to decide what you'd like to do most.
Outdoor activities are on offer during summer as well as winter, and our fantastic wildlife tours allow you to explore the natural environment of our many animals – a whale watching tour is only one of many possibilities.
If you love adventure, why not go on an adventure tour or visit one of our theme parks?

For lovers of culture, there are galleries, museums and fascinating exhibitions of Aboriginal art and history. Or if you prefer checking out the latest fashions, our shopping centres and markets are Australia's best.

You can experience everyday Australian life and stay in an apartment in the peaceful quiet countryside, or stay in a hotel in a city on the beach. Whatever you choose, you'll never forget your holiday in Queensland!

Your parents don't understand every word so they ask you about the article. Complete the dialogue.

You Schaut mal, was ich über Queensland im Internet gefunden habe!

Father Nicht schlecht ... Kann man dort Tiere beobachten?

You ______________________________ *(2 Dinge)*

Mother Ich bin ja eher für etwas Geschichte ...

You Das ist auch kein Problem. ______________________________

______________________________ *(2 Dinge)*

Father Gibt es auch etwas Spannenderes?

You Sicher! ______________________________ *(2 Dinge)*

Mother Ich würde ja auch gerne ein bisschen einkaufen gehen ...

You Das kannst du auch.

______________________________ *(2 Dinge)*

Father Wie sieht es denn mit einer Unterkunft aus?

You ______________________________ *(2 Dinge)*

Father Worauf warten wir dann noch? Auf geht's nach Australien!

WRITING

____/20

Feeling homesick

On the plane to Australia, Melanie met Aurélie, a girl from France. Aurélie is also an exchange student and is staying with a family on a farm near Melbourne.
The two girls often write e-mails to each other. In her last e-mail Aurélie was feeling very homesick and lonely. Write Melanie's reply (about 200 words).

You can include ...
- Melanie's own experience on the cattle farm,
- her feelings,
- questions about Aurélie's life and feelings,
- some advice.

E-Mails schreiben
- Benutze beim Verfassen deiner E-Mail **linking words** (after some time, suddenly, then, next, but, because, that, who ...), **beschreibende Adjektive** (an exciting trip) und **Adverbien** (I missed them terribly).
- Achte auf die Verwendung der richtigen Zeiten.
- Lies deine E-Mail am Ende noch einmal durch und korrigiere deinen Text.
- Weitere Tipps findest du in deinem Englischbuch auf S. 15 und im Skills File auf S. 144–145.

You can start like this:

Dear Aurélie,

I was very sorry to hear that you're not feeling so good at the moment.

___

___

___

___

___

___

___

___

___

___

___

SPEAKING

___/16

Bushfire!

As the climate in many parts of Australia is very dry and hot, every year there are many bushfires. These are dangerous for animals and for human beings.

Look at the statistics about bushfires in Australia and explain them. Start by giving a general picture of what the statistics show, then talk in more detail. Finish with a conclusion.

Informationen über Statistiken enthalten meist drei Teile:

1. Informationen darüber, was die Statistik zeigt: **The table is about ..., It shows the different ... in/of ... / It compares the size/number of ... with ...**
2. Genaue Beschreibungen und Erklärungen: **The chart/table compares the numbers of ..., x has the largest/second-largest/smallest ...**
3. Schlussfolgerungen: **So that shows that ..., You can see that ..., To conclude, you can say that ...**

Diese Übung passt zum Skills File auf S. 127 und zur Übung auf S. 10 in deinem Englischbuch. Du kannst die Übung auch schriftlich lösen.

Bushfire statistics – fires on public land in Victoria
Number of fires

Reasons for the fires	Average number of fires each year	Percentage of total[5] fires
Lightning[1]	149	26 %
Deliberate[2]	145	25 %
Agricultural[3]	96	16 %
Campfires	59	10 %
Cigarettes/Matches	41	7 %
Machinery/Exhausts[4]	15	3 %
Cause unknown	37	6 %
Other	42	8 %

Quelle: http://www.dse.vic.gov.au/fire-and-other-emergencies/fire-management/causes-of-bushfire/bushfire-statistics

You can start like this:

The table shows the different causes of bushfires in Victoria. It compares ...

[1] lightning ['laɪtnɪŋ] *Blitzeinschlag* [2] deliberate [dɪ'lɪbərət] *absichtlich, vorsätzlich*
[3] agricultural [ˌægrɪ'kʌltʃərəl] *landwirtschaftlich* [4] exhaust [ɪg'zɔːst] *Abgas* [5] total ['təʊtl] *Gesamt-*

Klassenarbeit B

Gesamtpunktzahl ohne Speaking	_____ / 50	Note	_____
Gesamtpunktzahl mit Speaking	_____ / 65	Note	_____

READING

_____ / 10

School of the Air Alice Springs

School of the Air Alice Springs – the world's largest classroom

Imagine life in a state where your nearest neighbour lives more than ten kilometres away from you, and the nearest town with a supermarket, cinema and school is a four-hour car-ride. Welcome to Central Australia!

The Alice Springs School of the Air (ASSOA) provides an educational service for about 120 children spread out across million square kilometres of Central Australia. They take part in lessons without having to come to a school building – they are educated by teachers via internet.

These children grow up in a special situation, because their nearest neighbour may live more than ten kilometres from their home. The next family with a child the same age may be as far as 200 km away, and the nearest school might be even further. This is why they need a different form of education.

In many ways the bush children clearly have an advantage over those living in a town or city. They are more active, healthier and freer than many other children. Most learn to ride horses at an early age, and they know how to survive in the outback. Many even know how to brand[1] a horse or cow, to crack a whip or even to drive a car. Others are familiar with Aboriginal traditions or regional plants and animals.

The School of the Air simply adds to this education, and brings in knowledge of the outside world. The students learn how to work independently and organize themselves.

All ASSOA students must have an identified tutor[2], and supervision[3] is required for a minimum of four hours per day.

The lessons at the School of the Air make learning an easier and happier process. This can be seen in the reaction of parents as well as students and their results in class tests. Students can stay at ASSOA until year 9. After that most move away from home to go to boarding school[4]. Years 3, 5 and 7 students are required to participate in the National Assessment Program (NAP)[5] each year. The school is in the top 10% of the education system in the Northern Territory.

[1] (to) brand [brændmɑːk] *brandmarken* [2] identified tutor [aɪˈdentɪfaɪd tjuːtə] *ausgewiesener Tutor (im Kontakt mit den Lehrern der ASSOA)* [3] supervision [ˌsuːpəˈvɪʒn] *Betreuung* [4] boarding school [ˈbɔːdɪŋ] *Internat*
[5] National Assessment Program: national testing of writing, reading and language skills to judge students' development

a) *Read the text carefully. Tick true, false or not given. (6P)*

	True	False	Not given
1 Children in the outback are less active than city children.			
2 There is no homework at the School of the Air.			
3 Outback children have special skills and know how to survive in the outback.			
4 The School of the Air provides lessons for about 120 students.			
5 Most of them travel a long distance to school every day.			
6 School of the Air students get better grades than students at normal schools.			

b) *Answer the questions with information from the text. (4P)*

1 Why is a School of the Air necessary in some parts of Australia?
2 Describe the communication between teachers and students at the School of the Air.
3 What advantages does the School of the Air offer the students?
4 Look at the text again. What do the students do after year 9?

LANGUAGE

___ / 25

1 WORDS Explaining words

___ / 7

Sometimes you do not know or you forgot how to say things in English. When that happens, you should use other words to describe what you are trying to say. In the following grid a student has started to explain some words. Help him finish his list!

Word	Explanation
independent	
	If you spend time in the sun you will develop this.
	It can be ~ to have a map when you visit a city you've never been to before.
conclusion	
	When you are in bed, you lie on this.
	If your brother thinks that your parents love you more than him, this is how he feels.
poison	

2 GRAMMAR Students at the School of the Air

_____ /5

Verb + object + *to*-infinitive
Nach einigen Verben kann ein Objekt stehen, auf das ein Infinitiv mit **to** folgt.
Präge dir diese Verben ein:
(to) ask sb. (not) to do sth.
(to) force sb. (not) to do sth.
(to) help sb. to do sth.
(to) teach sb. (not) to do sth.
(to) tell sb. (not) to do sth.
(to) want sb. to do sth.

Achtung! Nach den entsprechenden deutschen Verben steht ein Nebensatz mit „dass".
Auf die englischen Verben darf jedoch kein that-Satz folgen.

Complete the following interview with a student of the School of the Air.

Interviewer Why do you learn with the School of the Air?

Boy My parents ______________________________ (want – learn with) the School of the Air. There's no school near our house, so they thought it was a good idea for me.

Interviewer Can you describe school life to me and the listeners?

Boy Yes, of course. The computer is in our living room. We communicate via the internet, and the first thing I do in the morning is say hello to my classmates. Sometimes my little sister is still in the room, so I have to ______________________________. (tell – leave) Then, usually our teacher ______________________________ our homework. (want – read) Sometimes my father ______________________________ mathematical problems. (help – understand) He ______________________________ harder at school. (want – work) But that's quite difficult when there's nobody around to check if you're doing your school work.

Interviewer So being a student at the School of the Air is not always easy. Let's see what the next student has to say. Thanks for the interview!

Boy No worries!

3 GRAMMAR A new student at the School of the Air

___/5

Robert lives in a town one hundred kilometres away from Alice Springs. He is a new student at the School of the Air, and there are a lot of things he does not know about life at the school. Write down what he does not know or is unsure about using the ***to-infinitive****.*

I don't know I'm not sure	who where when how what	talk to on the first morning. get my student ID from. do my homework. hand in the assignments. say to my new classmates.

4 GRAMMAR The life of a School of the Air student

___/8

Twice a year a group of experienced students meets new students to welcome them. They talk about their lives at the School of the Air and answer questions the new students have. Re-write what they talk about using ***infinitives*** *instead of relative clauses.*

1 There is a lot of work which we have to do over the weekend.

___

___

2 There are different assignments that we have to complete.

___

___

3 We have a teacher who takes care of the new students.

___

4 During the break I go and see my mum in the kitchen where I can have a cup of tea.

___

___

5 I'm happy that there is no uniform which I have to wear.

___

6 I am the first person in my family who has come to Australia as an exchange student.

___

___

7 We had nobody who we could ask for help.

___

8 At the beginning there are a lot of new things that you have to learn.

___

___

WRITING

___ /15

Australian Aborigines

A sad and often unknown part of Australia's history is the story of the Aborigines or Aboriginals. You have decided to write a report about the Australian Aborigines for your school magazine.

Use the fact sheet below to write your text.

past:
- 40,000 years ago developed oldest rock art in the world
- 19th century: Aborigines had to move because of European settlers; Aborigines who did not go were killed
- Europeans thought Aborigine culture was primitive
- Number of Aborigines reduced
- 1963: right to vote for Aborigines
- Until 1970s: Aboriginal children taken away from families

today:
- Australia's population: more than 20 million, approx. 2% Aborigines
- Some still don't live in the same place their whole lives, move around within a limited area, some live in tribes
- Oldest members make decisions
- Problems: discrimination, poverty, too much alcohol, unemployment

Sachtexte schreiben
- Verfasse deinen Sachtext nüchtern und ohne Spannung hineinzubringen (zum Beispiel durch ausschmückende Adjektive). Verwende dennoch **linking words** (**but**, **because**, **after** *...)*, um Sätze zu verbinden.
- Denke an die Verwendung der richtigen Zeit!
- Verwende keine Kurzformen (**do not** anstatt **don't**).

SPEAKING

___ /15

I can tell you more

a) *Find yourself a partner and act out the role play together.*

Imagine you're staying at a campsite on the east coast of Australia. You meet an Australian boy/girl who is staying in the caravan next to yours.

Start your conversation very politely and introduce yourselves. Ask and answer questions. Ask for help if you need to or give help if you are asked. End your conversation in a friendly way. Take ten minutes to prepare your dialogue.

Sprechen üben
- Du und dein Partner könnt euch gegenseitig korrigieren, so funktioniert die Übung am besten.
- Du kannst den Dialog aber auch jeweils nur für Partner A oder B aufnehmen und mit der Aufnahme jeweils die andere Rolle einsprechen und aufzeichnen. So kannst du dich selbst überprüfen und korrigieren.

Partner A: the German boy/girl

- you arrived the evening before
- you're from Frankfurt am Main
- you go camping every year
- it's your first time at this campsite
- you want to find out more about the campsite (pool? / disco? / café? / how far to the beach?)
- you're interested in swimming in the sea

Partner B: the Australian boy/girl

- you arrived 10 days ago
- you're from Alice Springs, Northern Territory, Australia
- you love camping
- it's the third time you've been to the campsite, weather always great
- you know a lot (pool ▸ near the entrance, café at campsite, opposite supermarket, disco ▸ outside the campsite once a week on Friday ▸ five minutes' walk)
- you want to go to the beach in half an hour

b) *Swap roles and imagine you both really hate camping and it's raining cats and dogs. Create a dialogue of the same length as in* ***a)*** *with your partner.*

Partner A: the German boy/girl

- you arrived the evening before
- you are from Chemnitz
- you go camping every year (your first time at this campsite)
- you prefer staying in hotels
- you want to know which cities your partner likes
- you enjoy holidays at the sea because you like swimming and eating fish

Partner B: the Australian boy/girl

- you arrived ten days ago
- you are from Cardiff in Wales
- this is your third time at the campsite
- weather has been bad so far
- you hate camping
- you like hotels (say why)
- you prefer going to different places every year (e.g. Paris, Barcelona, Vienna)
- you want to have an ice-cream

Klassenarbeit A

Gesamtpunktzahl ohne Speaking	______ / 97	Note ______
Gesamtpunktzahl mit Speaking	______ / 110	Note ______

READING

______ / 5

Different jobs for different people

Read the following job adverts from the Springfield News of February 21st. Then answer the questions.

Retail[1] staff wanted

Work is available in our new department stores and boutiques throughout the country. Most positions are as sales assistants, however there are also stock-taking[2] jobs. For retail you need fluent English. Experience is helpful but not necessary.

We need help especially in the months leading up to Christmas – particularly in our department stores.

Apply within one of our stores or call Steven at 0207 – 324567 and ask for an appointment for an interview.

Fashcloth Ltd. The Fashion Stores

Call centre agent

If you have sales experience and love to talking to people, this could be the job for you. In most positions you have to make phone calls to sell one of our products. You will need to speak English fluently and be confident about your sales skills. Positions are usually parttime. We offer a great salary (£12 per hour plus bonuses for sales).

Don't hesitate[3] to send your application and CV via email to staff@callyou.co.uk.

Callyou Call Centres. Any questions?

Help us harvest

Our apples are one of the most delicious fruits in the world. At Fruitco Bournemouth, we take extra care that their great taste is guaranteed. For the new harvesting season, we need you to help us pick the ripe fruit so that it can be delivered to our valued customers around the world.

However, it is hard physical work and – even in England – sometimes in hot weather.
As we pay you by the amount you pick, you'll earn more as you become more experienced.

Send an application to *Fruitco*, 893A Castle Lane West, Bournemouth, Dorset BH8 9UA.

1 Where will you earn more money the more successful you are?

____

2 Which job do you need to have experience for?

____

3 What kind of jobs is the department store offering?

____

4 What do you have to be prepared for when you work as an apple picker?

____

5 What qualifications do you need to have when you work in a call centre?

____

[1] retail [ri:teɪl] *Einzelhandel* [2] stock-taking [stɒkteɪkɪŋ] *Inventur* [3] (to) hesitate ['hezɪteɪt] *zögern*

WRITING

___/20

Applying for a job

*Choose **a)** or **b)**.*

***a)** Apply for one of the jobs described in the adverts in the reading exercise. Write an application letter. Write something about your skills and why you would be the right person for this job.*

***b)** Sue Evans lives in Bristol. She has seen the advert below and wants to apply for the job. Write her application letter. Write something about her skills and why she would be the right person for this job.*

Förmliche Briefe *(formal letters)*
- Adresse ohne Namen
- vollständige Anschrift
- Datum
- höfliche Anrede
- Langformen verwenden
- Brief in Absätze gliedern
- Ende: Dank im Voraus, höfliche Schlussformel, Unterschrift, getippter Name

Einen Beispielbrief findest du im Skills File auf S.146 in deinem Englischbuch.

The Bristol Times 2 November 2011

St. John's Residential Care Home[1]

At St. John's we have 80 residents[2] and consider it extremely important to offer each one of them a wide range of free-time activities.

We are looking for a **young volunteer** (m/f) to teach a small group (12 people) basic computer skills, including using the internet and writing e-mails.
The classes would take place once a week for one hour. If you know how to use the internet effectively and know a bit about downloading programs and how to surf the internet safely, you are the right person for this job! And don't be afraid – you don't have to be an internet expert to apply, but you should be able to explain things so that your "students" find their way round the internet.

Are you interested in working with people and sharing your IT skills?
We would provide training after Christmas.
Please tell us which days of the week would suit you best.

Sorry, we can't pay anything, but we will be happy to give you a reference.
Please send your application letter plus CV to:

Ms Alice Spring
St. John's Residential Care Home
4 New Garden Street, Bristol BS1 3AD

[1] Residential Care Home [ˌrezɪˈdenʃl keə(r) həʊm] *Pflegeheim* [2] resident [ˈrezɪdənt] *Bewohner/in, Anwohner/in*

LANGUAGE

____/51

1 WORDS Jobs

____/21

a) *Make a mind map for the topic "jobs". Use the new vocabulary from Unit 2.*
The numbers tell you how many words you should be able to add to each word group.
You can add more words as you work through the unit. (17P)

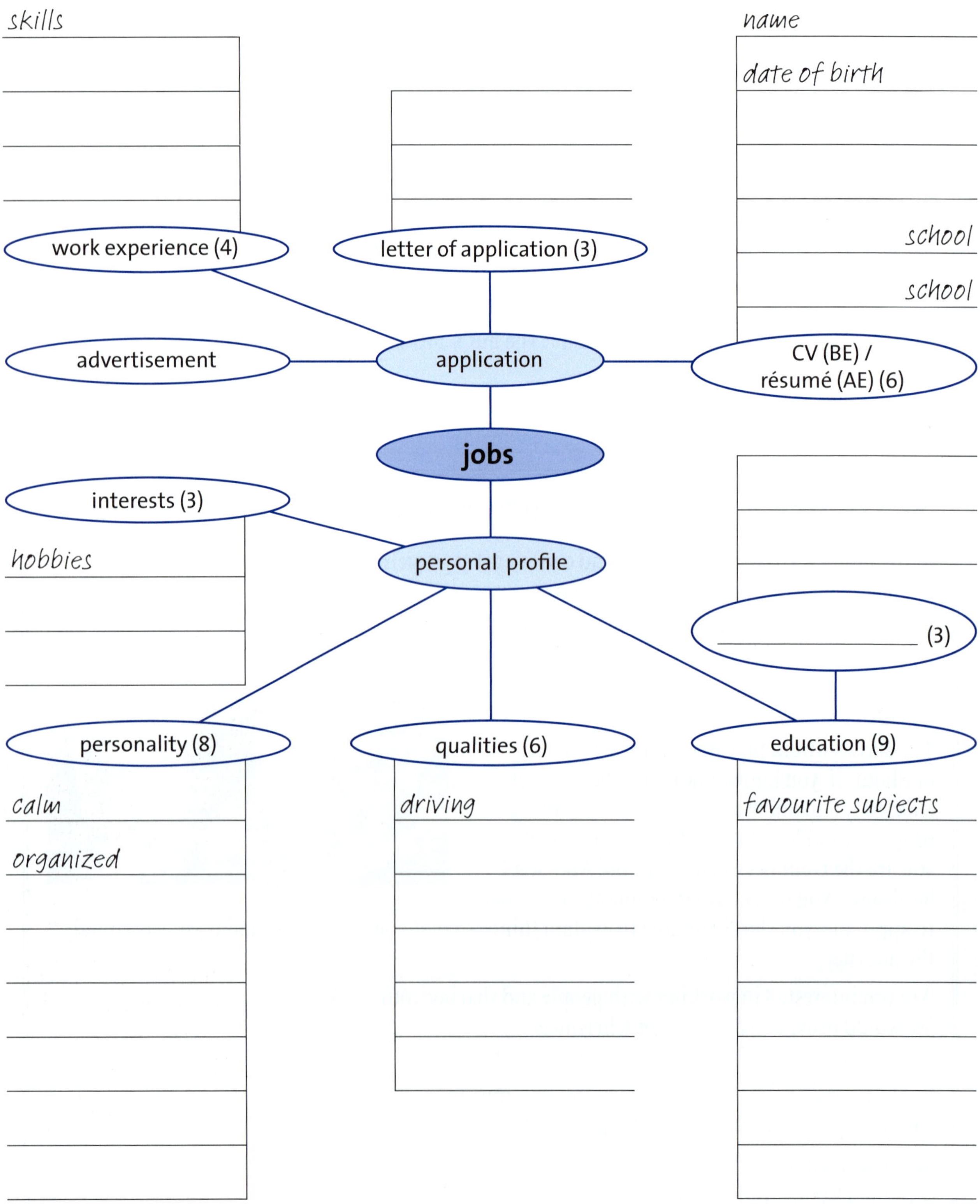

b) *Choose **four** words from your mind map and write sentences for each one in your exercise book. (4P)*

2 WORDS Nigel's nightmare of getting a job

___ /5

Nigel has written twenty applications for almost every job advert he could find, but so far he has only received letters of rejection[1].

Re-write his thoughts using ***negative prefixes****.*

1 Sometimes I have the feeling that it is *not possible* to get the perfect job.

____

2 So far I have*n't* been *lucky* in finding a job.

____

3 I did*n't* feel very *comfortable* at my last interview.

____

4 It would*n't* be *polite* to tell the manager that you think his tie looks awful.

____

5 You take a big risk[2] if you apply for a job and your CV is*n't accurate*.

____

3 GRAMMAR This is me!

___ /10

Complete Timmy's description by using the words in the box below. Use ***gerunds****.*

do (2x) • eat • get • go • hang • lead • listen to • play • ride

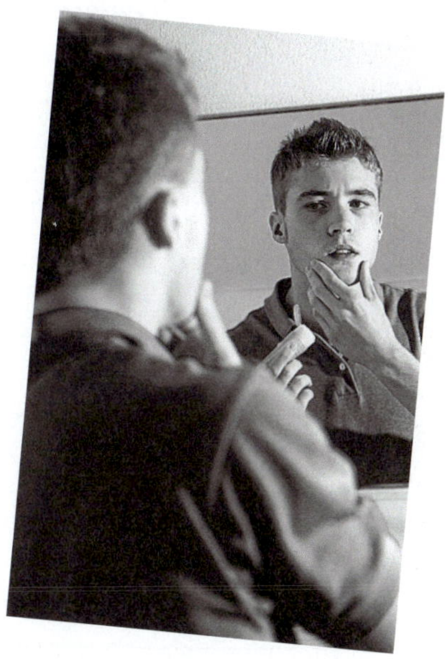

My name is Timmy and I am good at ______________ football and ______________ other people's problems. At least this is what people say. I like ______________ to the cinema with my best friend Tony. ______________ around with friends from school is great fun! ______________ a healthy life is also important for me. I stay fit by ______________ lots of sports and ______________ all my vegetables. I am keen on ______________ my scooter. I'm always very serious about environmental issues[3] without ______________ involved in politics. After I leave school, I want to study law and become a judge. Well, what else ...? Ah, yes. What I don't like is ______________ homework. It ruins my whole day, I can tell you.

[1] rejection [rɪ'dʒekʃn] *Absage, Ablehung* [2] risk [rɪsk] *Risiko* [3] issue ['ɪʃuː] *Thema, Problem*

4 WORDS Translating „Möglichkeit"

In German, all of the following sentences contain the word „Möglichkeiten". Choose the correct English expression.

1 Have you had the ______________________________ to contact the job agency yet?

2 There are a number of ______________________________ to apply for a job.

3 Have you thought of the ______________________________ of asking for a job in the shop?

4 The ______________________ of getting a job without an interview are very small indeed.

5 There is no ______________________________ of getting to this place without a car.

6 We have the ____________________ of going to Madame Tussaud's when we are in London.

5 GRAMMAR Things the employer tells you

_____/9

*The manager of the company at which you applied for a job tells you a lot about working there. Write what he says. Use **gerunds**.*

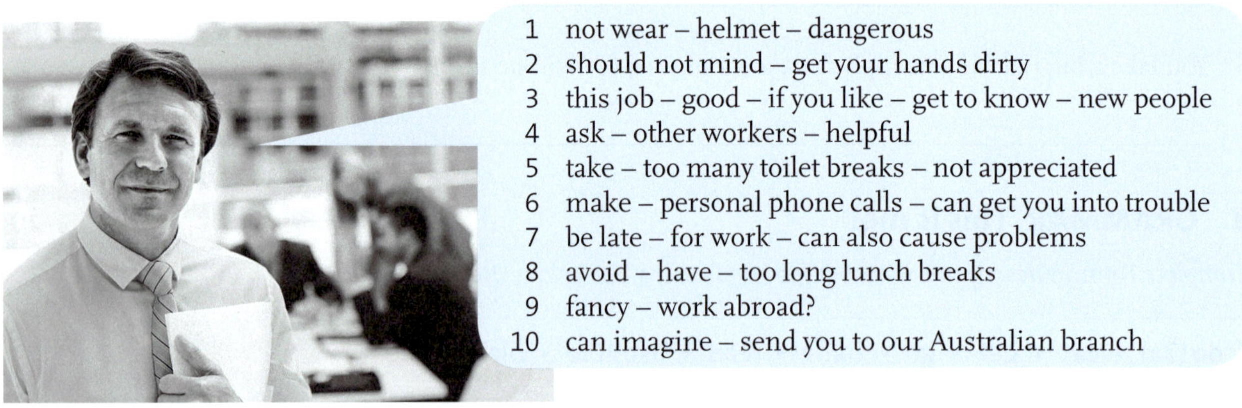

1 *Not wearing a helmet is dangerous.*

2 ______________________________

3 ______________________________

4 ______________________________

5 ______________________________

6 ______________________________

7 ______________________________

8 ______________________________

9 ______________________________

10 ______________________________

Mehr Übungen zu **gerunds** und **infinitives** findest du in Klassenarbeit B.

STUDY SKILLS

____ / 21

Getting a scholarship[1] for the USA

Imagine you want to spend a year in the USA but you haven't got enough money to do that.

Fortunately, there are organizations which support young students who wish to study abroad by offering them a scholarship. To apply for this, you need to send in a formal application letter as well as your CV, which should give an insight into your activities at school and your extracurricular activities. Write your CV.

Einen Lebenslauf schreiben

- Name, Adresse, Telefonnummer, E-Mail-Adresse
- Personal statement, in dem du dich kurz beschreibst
- Lückenlose Darstellung deiner schulischen Laufbahn und erworbener Abschlüsse
- Auflistung deiner beruflichen Laufbahn, z. B. Praktika, Ferienjobs
- Deine Fähigkeiten, Hobbys, Interessen
- Kurse oder Preise
- Angabe außerschulischer Aktivitäten und Qualifikationen, z. B. Schülersprecher, Trainer

Der Lebenslauf wird nicht unterschrieben. Ein Bild gehört zwar nicht unbedingt dazu, wird aber oft im Rahmen der Bewerbungsunterlagen gefordert.
Ein Beispiel für einen Lebenslauf findest du auf S. 38 in deinem Englischbuch, Tipps auf S. 148.

[1] scholarship ['skɒləʃɪp] *Stipendium*

SPEAKING

____/13

03 An assessment centre – Part 1

Think of a job you would like to apply for. Imagine you sent an application and a CV to the company.
A few days later you received a message on your answer-phone. The manager of the company called you and suggested two possible dates. Listen to what he says.

04 Now you

Call the company to confirm the date and ask for further information.
Press "pause" when you hear the beep. Press "play" when you've said your part.

1 ***The manager of Boxcom and partners***
▼

You Sage wer du bist, bedanke dich für die Nachricht und frage nach, ob es sich um ein Assessment Center oder ein Vorstellungsgespräch handelt. (3P)

2 ***Manager***
▼

You Sage, dass du nicht genau weißt, was ein Assessment Center ist und frage nach einer Erläuterung. (2P)

3 ***Manager***
▼

You Frage, ob du es richtig verstanden hast, dass die erfolgreiche Teilnahme am Assessment Center die Voraussetzung für eine Einladung zu einem Vorstellungsgespräch ist. (2P)

4 ***Manager***
▼

You Bestätige den Termin und frage nach der genauen Adresse. (2P)

5 ***Manager***
▼

You Sage, dass das unproblematisch ist. Du kennst den Weg dorthin. Du hast keine weiteren Fragen. (3P)

6 ***Manager***
▼

You Bedanke dich. (1P)

7 ***Manager***
▼

Gesamtpunktzahl ohne Speaking	____ / 59	Note ____
Gesamtpunktzahl mit Speaking	____ / 73	Note ____

LISTENING

____ / 22

05

Are you happy with your job?

The radio programme Radio Today has a themed week on the topic "Are you happy with your job". Each morning between 10 and 11 another person is interviewed.

a) *Read the sentences carefully. Then listen to Terry and Alice. Are the statements true or false? Correct the wrong sentences. (11P)*

	True	False	Why
1 Alice hasn't always been happy with her job, but her career is going well now.			
2 Alice doesn't like her job because she doesn't have much free time anymore.			
3 Alice knew from the start what she wanted to do after school.			
4 After school Alice started to work at her father's computer shop.			
5 Alice worked in a supermarket and thought about her interests.			
6 Alice has a boutique with one of her friends now.			
7 Alice has made her hobby her job.			

→

06 ***b)*** *Listen to Terry and Harry. Then tick a), b), c) or d). (5P)*

1 After finishing school Harry ...	a) did secretarial jobs.	
	b) did some work experience.	
	c) worked in a supermarket.	
	d) spent a year abroad.	

2 Harry became a careers advisor because ...	a) this was his dream job.	
	b) he got the chance to do some special training.	
	c) he didn't know what else to do.	
	d) he had had many problems in finding the perfect job himself.	

3 Harry works only part-time as a careers advisor because ...	a) he decided to find out about his strengths.	
	b) he doesn't need the money.	
	c) he decided to focus on his book.	
	d) he has to travel a lot to give interviews about his book.	

4 Harry likes his job very much because ...	a) he can work at home.	
	b) he gives other people advice and makes them happy.	
	c) he gets to know a lot of people.	
	d) he gets nice presents from the readers of his book.	

5 Harry wrote the book because ...	a) he wanted to help young people through the jungle of job applications.	
	b) he wanted to become a successful author.	
	c) he found his job boring and wanted to try something different.	
	d) he wanted to give young people advice about job interviews.	

c) *Listen to Harry's tips and complete the table.*
Write down three tips each about what applicants should do and should not do. (6P)

Shoulds	**Should nots**
______________________	______________________
______________________	______________________
______________________	______________________
______________________	______________________
______________________	______________________
______________________	______________________

LANGUAGE

_____/25

1 WORDS The downside of being rich

_____/9

Michael H. (17) has made a fortune by creating webpages for big companies. Here he tells you why being rich is not always a blessing.

Read his text and fill in the correct word from the box in the correct form.

(to) advise • ambition • calm • confident • design • determination • (to) determine • employee • faith in • (to) focus • fortune • greedy • (to) impress • necessary • responsible • stressful • university • within

It all started because I wanted to ______________ my classmates at school. I have always been interested in computers and games, so I decided to ______________ on creating websites for companies. At my uncle's birthday party I met a guy who was successful in that kind of work, and he ______________ me to concentrate on special ______________ which nobody had ever done before. I was ______________ to start my own business and so I decided not to go to ______________. I told my parents that it wasn't ______________ for me to study and to my great surprise they stayed ______________. The more pages I created, the more my ______________ grew and my ______________ to achieve more. I was ______________ for my own projects! My little business became very successful and I soon needed ______________. My ______________ myself increased and I became more ______________. I thought I could make my ______________ in this business. However, ______________ a few months I lost something which I had never enjoyed as much as I could: I realized I wasn't a child anymore. I was leading the ______________ life of a ______________ adult!

2 GRAMMAR Stop being lazy and get a job

____/9

Nigel was eventually successful with one of his applications and he got invited to a job interview. He is so excited about it! Read his thoughts and use the correct form of the verbs to make correct sentences.

Nach den Verben **to forget, to remember, to stop** und **to try** kann sowohl ein Gerundium als auch ein **to**-Infinitiv stehen. Beachte dabei die unterschiedlichen Bedeutungen.

I ______________________ (remember, talk) to my teacher about applications last year. He told me to ______________________ (stop, make) so many mistakes in my application letters. I tried really hard, but he still always found a lot of mistakes in the applications I showed him. I'll never ______________________ (forget, listen) to all the feedback he gave me. For practice, I ______________________ (tried, write) as many applications as I could. And I even ______________________ (stop, play) football with my friends or ____________ (go) to the cinema with them after school. I also improved my CV. One day I sent an application to a company. I was very nervous and in the meantime I even ______________________ (try, do) yoga to calm myself down. One week later I got a letter and now I have a job interview, I'm so happy! I mustn't ______________________ (forget, call) my mother after the interview and I must ______________________(remember, say) thank you to my teacher.

3 GRAMMAR We want you!

____/7

Read this notice from a school's notice board. Take one preposition and one verb from the box and complete the text. Be careful: there is one more preposition and one more verb than you need.

Nach einer **Präposition (by, for, of, without, ...)** folgt das Verb als **Gerundium**.

about • at • in (2x) • of (2x) • on • to
be • earn • explain • help • spend • talk • teach • write

Are you interested ______________________ some extra money?

Are you used ______________________ your favourite subject to other students?

Are you interested ______________________ exercises?

Are you good ______________________ ideas and concepts?

Are you keen ______________________ younger students from your school?

Are you tired ______________________ afternoons alone?

Do you dream ______________________ a teacher?

Then join our school's homework club and help younger students in your favourite subject!
For further information ask Mr Lee.

MEDIATION

___/12

A job for your exchange partner

Your exchange partner Pete from England is staying with you for the summer holidays. He has found an advert for a summer job but doesn't understand everything, so he asks you to explain some things to him.

Read the advert, then answer your partner's questions in English on page 32.

Aushilfe in der Touristeninformation gesucht!

Jedes Jahr kommen Tausende Besucher aus allen Ländern der Erde nach Stuttgart. Hier finden sie Erholung, attraktive Freizeitangebote und ein breites Spektrum an Einkaufsmöglichkeiten. Nicht zuletzt sind auch unsere hervorragenden Restaurants ein beliebtes Ziel für Liebhaber saisonaler Küche.

Für die Zeit der Sommerferien suchen wir deshalb eine englischsprachige Aushilfe in unserer Touristeninformation für unsere Gäste aus den USA. Sie müssen nicht unbedingt über Erfahrungen im Tourismus verfügen und auch keine Kenntnisse über unsere Stadt mitbringen.

Ihre Aufgaben werden sein, Touristen am Flughafen zu begrüßen und ihnen ein Informationsblatt auszuhändigen. In der Touristeninformation werden Sie dann alle englischen Fragen an unsere ausgebildeten Mitarbeiter weitergeben. Ihre Arbeitszeit ist montags bis samstags von 9.00 bis 18:30 Uhr.

Wir erwarten von Ihnen ein sicheres Auftreten sowie hervorragende Englischkenntnisse. Pünktlichkeit und Zuverlässigkeit sind darüber hinaus selbstverständlich.

Wir bieten Ihnen einen überdurchschnittlichen Verdienst von € 12,00 pro Stunde.

Interesse? Dann schauen Sie doch einfach direkt in der Touristeninformation am Marktplatz vorbei und fragen Sie dort nach Frau Eigel.

Tourismusverband Stuttgart
0711 – 34 56 78.

→

Pete Well, this is the advert I found in the newspaper. What kind of job is it exactly?

You ____

____

Pete And what do I have to do? *(three things)*

You ____

____

Pete That sounds good to me. But don't I have to know the area for this job?

You ____

____

Pete But what skills do I need? *(three things)*

You ____

____

Pete When do I have to work?

You ____

____

Pete But I'm only here for the summer holidays.

You ____

____

Pete OK then. How can I apply for it? *(two things)*

You ____

____

SPEAKING

____/14

An assessment centre – Part 2

Now you arrive at the Boxcom assessment centre. The first task is to give a presentation for five minutes about yourself, your skills and why you applied for this job.

Make notes for your speech and practise it. If possible, record it and check your results.

☞ **Sprechen üben**
Auch beim Sprechen solltest du dich kontrollieren. Du kannst deinen Vortrag aufnehmen oder eine andere Person bitten, deinen Vortrag anzuhören und dir später eine Rückmeldung zu geben.
Achte auf:
- Gliederung des Vortrags,
- korrekte Zeitformen,
- flüssiges Sprechen.

You can use the following table for your preparation.

Personal information	Name:
	Age:
	City in which you live:
Education	
What your interests are (should have something to do with the job)	
What your skills are (should have something to do with the job)	
Why you applied for the job	
What makes you the best person for the job	

Klassenarbeit A

Gesamtpunktzahl ohne Speaking	_____ / 104	Note _____
Gesamtpunktzahl mit Speaking	_____ / 116	Note _____

LISTENING

_____ / 30

07 I love my city!

Abdel, Tin-Mi and Ranjid are new students at an international school. Their teacher has asked them to say a few words about where they are from and what they think about their home town.

Listen to what they tell their class. Then complete the table.

	 **Abdel**	 **Tin-Mi**	 **Ranjid**
Place			
General information about the city			
Positive aspects (+)			
Negative aspects (–)			

LANGUAGE

____/45

1 WORDS Big city life

____/30

***a)** Complete the table with words about city life. (17P)*

Positive aspects	Negative aspects	Places	Buildings	________	Verbs	Adjectives
________	poverty	suburb	football	airport	attract	urban
________	________	________	________	________	________	________
________	________	________	hotel	________	________	________
________	________	________	________	________	________	________
________	________	________	________			________
________	________					________
________	________					________
	________					

***b)** Now complete the following sentences using the correct words from the table. (13P)*

1 In my city all the walls are covered with ________________.

2 In the summer holidays, we usually take the ________________ to the ________________.

3 Next Saturday my favourite team is playing in our ________________.

4 There are some ________________ buildings in our city, but there are also some ________________, very tall ________________ in the ________________ area where the major banks are situated.

5 When you take the ________________ out of the city, you quickly reach a beautiful ________________ area.

6 One of the reasons why many cities are ________________ is they don't have effective systems to deal with waste.

7 There is a lot of ________________ in my city and a lot of people are homeless. They have to sleep on the streets.

8 The ________________ rate is high. Every day there are reports of burglaries and street shootings. As a tourist you should beware of pickpockets on the tram.

2 WORDS My city is beautiful

___/5

A reporter for the school's magazine asks Ranjid what's so interesting about Mumbai. This is what he says.

*Help him find the correct **suffix** to make a fitting adjective for each sentence.*

In my opinion, Mumbai isn't the most beaut________ city in the world. There are a lot of nois________ and smell________ cars, which cause a lot of people sleep________ nights. When the noise gets too pain________, you can leave the city and relax in the end________ fields which spread out around it. The movie business is a tradition________ and very power________ industry here and it attracts a lot of money to the city. However, there are still quite a few home________ people in the city. There are so many contrasts in Mumbai, it's the most interesting city imagin________.

3 WORDS Kung-fu fighting in Hong Kong

___/6

Tin-Mi is back in Hong Kong for her holidays. As a kung-fu fan, she goes to see some fights.
Here she talks about the experience.

*Improve the style of the sentences for a radio report by using **participles as adjectives**.*

> **Participles as adjectives**
> Du kannst diese Übung in drei Schritten bearbeiten:
> 1. Markiere den **Relativsatz**.
> 2. Identifiziere darin **Adjektive** und **Verben** und forme diese um zu einem zusammengesetzten Adjektiv (**compound adjective**).
> 3. Verbessere den Satz.

1 It was amazing that there were so many people who speak Chinese at the fights.

____

2 At the beginning of the competition, a young man who looked strong entered the ring.

____

3 His opponent was an old man who was educated well.

____

4 At the end, the champion, who had fought hard, was given a prize.

____

5 It may not look like it, but kung-fu is a sport for people who are able to move fast.

____

6 Although it is a fight, most kung-fu fighters are people who love peace.

____

4 GRAMMAR Townships in Cape Town

____ /4

Abdel has to give a short talk to his English class about the poverty in Cape Town.

Here are some key words which he has noted down. Make complete sentences using ***present participles****.*

1. Although – rich people and nice areas in Cape Town – tourists still see – a lot of people – hang around – in the streets
2. There are – a lot of people – live in slums
3. In the townships – you can see – children – play – in front of houses which are falling down
4. On some tours – tourists listen to – people – play traditional music

The present participle after certain verbs

- Nach Verben der Wahrnehmung, z.B. **feel**, **hear**, **listen to**, **notice**, **see**, **smell**, **watch**, folgt ein Objekt sowie das Partizip Präsens: I **heard** the baby **crying** next door.
- Weitere Beispiele findest du im Grammar File 3.3 auf S. 158 in deinem Englischbuch.

1 ______________________________

____

2 ______________________________

3 ______________________________

____

4 ______________________________

WRITING

____/ 29

Landslide hits an orphanage

a) *Read this newspaper article and then look at the language and structure. What elements make the text subjective? Write five things in your exercise book. (5P)*

Landslide[1] hits orphanage[2] – six children dead

Six children lost their lives today when a landslide hit an orphanage in a peaceful village near Mumbai. "I heard a loud noise and suddenly I was covered in earth and dust. I had to run for my life," said eye-witness Terki Suleiman.

Hundreds of rescue workers tried their best to find survivors, but after five hours searching they had only found dead bodies.

"I was the one who found the first child," said Andy McDowell, a volunteer with the Red Cross in India. "I couldn't stop crying. I just can't believe what happened here."

Not all the bodies have been found yet, but six children aged eight to ten are believed to have lost their lives in the landslide. The boy found by McDowell was taken to hospital immediately, but he could not be saved. "It was too late for him," Martin Andrews, a doctor at the Red Cross Hospital Mumbai, explained. "When I examined him, I couldn't do anything more for him."

The landslide is a disaster for the orphanage, which is in a poor region of India. Three adults, who were working at the orphanage, are also reported missing.

Local charities and this newspaper had warned officials that the orphanage buildings were not safe and that there might be a catastrophe. But they were not listened to! Now it is the children who have to pay the price!

It was still raining when our reporter arrived at the scene. "This terrible rain is preventing us from trying to rescue the missing boys and girls," McDowell told us. More than 100 officials, firefighters and volunteers from the Red Cross stood in a circle unable to believe what had happened. "The children were having their dinner when the mud fell over them," said Geraldine Guetta, manager of the orphanage, wiping away her tears. "The roof couldn't carry the heavy load and collapsed, burying the children underneath it. They didn't have time to escape."

Nearby buildings have been evacuated as officials fear another landslide tonight.

[1] landslide ['lænddslaɪd] *Erdrutsch* [2] orphanage ['ɔːfənɪdʒ] *Waisenhaus*

b) *Write a* ***summary*** *of the article in your exercise book. (13P)*

Summary writing
1. **Markiere** alle **wichtigen Fakten**, die dir Antworten auf die **Wh-Fragen** geben **(Who? What? Where? When? Why?)** und halte sie in **Stichpunkten** fest.
2. **Klammere unwichtige Details**, Adjektive, rhetorische Fragen, wörtliche Rede und persönliche Kommentare **ein**. Diese gehören nicht in die Summary.
3. Stelle dir vor, du müsstest **jemandem, der den Text nicht gelesen hat**, erklären, worum es darin geht: Fasse den Text **in eigenen Worten** zusammen und verwende **simple present**.

Weitere Hilfen findest du im Skills File auf S. 149 in deinem Englischbuch.

c) *Re-write the text as an* ***objective report*** *in your exercise book. (16P)*

Writing a report
1. Erwähne in einem einleitenden, **zusammenfassenden Satz**, was passiert ist.
2. Nenne erst die wichtigen Informationen und anschließend die Details. Dabei kannst du dich an den **Wh-Fragen (Who? What? Where? When? Why?)** orientieren.
3. Schreibe deinen Bericht im **simple past**, ohne reißerische Adjektive oder direkte Rede. Es geht lediglich um eine **nüchterne und sachliche Darstellung von Fakten**. Schildere das Geschehen, ohne es zu kommentieren.

SPEAKING

____/12

08 Booking a holiday

Sarah wants to book herself a holiday and calls a travel agency. Listen to the conversation.

Note down useful phrases which you could use to book a holiday by telephone.

09 Now you

Now imagine you want to book a language holiday for yourself at an English language school.

You ...
- would like to go to Brighton for two weeks in your summer holidays, starting on the 21st June, to relax on the beach and learn English.
- would like to take the train.
- need accommodation (bed & breakfast).
- don't mind homestay accommodation in a host family, if this can be organized by the language school.
- would like to stay two weeks in Brighton.
- cannot pay more than 800 pounds in total.

Make the phone call. Press 'pause' when you hear the beep, press 'play' when you've said your part.

Klassenarbeit B

Gesamtpunktzahl ______ / 68 Note ______

READING

______ / 31

Read this article taken from the educational section of an American newspaper. Then complete the task below.

Too many violent students at schools in big cities

School teachers address parents for help

For many teachers the situation in the classroom has become more and more difficult in recent years. "My students tend to be more aggressive than they used to be," says Ann Smith, a math teacher at Highland College in Boston. "Hardly a day goes by without doors being slammed, fire crackers being thrown or pictures being torn from the walls. At break I watch students beating each other up or using the trash cans as footballs."

In some families both parents are unemployed and the children are the only members of the family who have to get up before lunchtime. "This is especially a problem in big cities," says Anne Perfew, an educational advisor, working with schools in Massachusetts. "In rural areas, teachers don't report having these kinds of problems with their students."

Mike Liberty, a sports and math teacher at a small town college 50 miles west of Boston, does not face the kind of difficulties his colleagues have to deal with at schools in the big cities. "We had some major discussions when one of our students was caught smoking in the school yard. But we don't have problems with young people smashing doors or attacking fellow students."

A solution to this problem can only be found if schools and parents work together. "These days in our cities it has become more important than ever for parents, as 'education consumers', to know about the school's ideas and concepts but also about their rights and responsibilities and those of their children," says principal Mike Tannors. Parents cannot simply rely on the school's newsletter or occasional conversations with one or two of the teachers or 'education distributors'. As he puts it, parents often seem to know their mechanic better than their kids' teachers. "If children were cars, their owners would be a lot better informed about their options – they would check on safety features, new innovations and ask about the best value for their money."

For most children there is just a small window during which they can learn the most important rules and values to behave correctly in public and get their educational basics right. "It is important for parents to assist by keeping this small window of opportunity open. By helping their children behave better, they help them learn better too," says Perfew.

The uncertainty regarding the right approach to take is felt by teachers and parents alike and shows that both sides need help. The millions of US dollars spent each year on books and magazines giving educational help and advice also point to an interest in this subject. The popularity of reality television shows like 'Super nanny' shows parents' urgent need for educational advice, no matter if the sources of that advice may be open to criticism.

The relationship between teachers and parents is often characterized by prejudices. Parents find it difficult to trust teachers because of their own bad experiences; teachers lose faith in parents because they feel that they are not getting the necessary support from them. This obviously harms an efficient cooperation between the two sides involved. The situation would certainly be much easier if parents and teachers cooperated more for the benefit of the child's education.

a) *Complete the sentences in your own words. (10P)*

1 In the text, teachers are described as 'education distributors', so parents can be seen as

____.

2 More and more students are acting aggressively at school. They ______________________

____.

3 In some families the children ____

____.

4 Students do not only beat each other up, they also ______________________________

____.

5 It is important that parents understand ______________________________ and know

____.

6 If children were cars, parents ____.

7 Parents' relationship to their car mechanic ______________________________________

____.

8 The fact that parents need advice about the education of their offspring is shown

____.

9 It would be much easier if ____

____.

10 In order to achieve this both sides ____.

b) *Write a summary of the article. (10P)*

Tipps zum **Summary writing** findest du auf S. 39.

c) *Should parents be more involved in their children's school life?* ***Comment*** *in about 100 words. (11P)*

Einen Kurzkommentar schreiben

In einem Kurzkommentar beziehst du Stellung zu einem Zitat oder einer (manchmal provokanten) These. Es geht nicht darum, zu erraten, was deine Lehrerin oder dein Lehrer gern hören möchte – **deine eigene Meinung** ist gefragt!

- Überlege dir eine **These** und stütze diese mit einem **Argument**.
- Nenne ein **Gegenargument** und versuche dieses mit deinen Argumenten zu entkräften: **On the one hand ..., on the other hand ...** .
- Schreibe auch zu kurzen Texten eine **Einleitung** und einen zusammenfassenden **Schlusssatz**.

LANGUAGE

___/25

1 WORDS A crossword

___/13

Complete the crossword with the correct words.

Across

1 A person who travels from home to work every day.

3 When you're on holiday, this can help you to find your way around.

5 A room has a floor, four walls and a … .

7 Houses are usually built using this material.

9 Almost all the seats were taken. Sarah was the last person to … one.

11 A person who illegally occupies a flat or house.

13 An attractive smell.

Down

2 If it's hot in your room, you can use this to cool down.

4 Clothes you wear under your regular clothes.

6 A prisoner is kept in a … .

8 If you look into the distance, the place the earth and sky meet is the … .

10 A newspaper article is usually printed in … .

12 A poor person who asks people for money in the street.

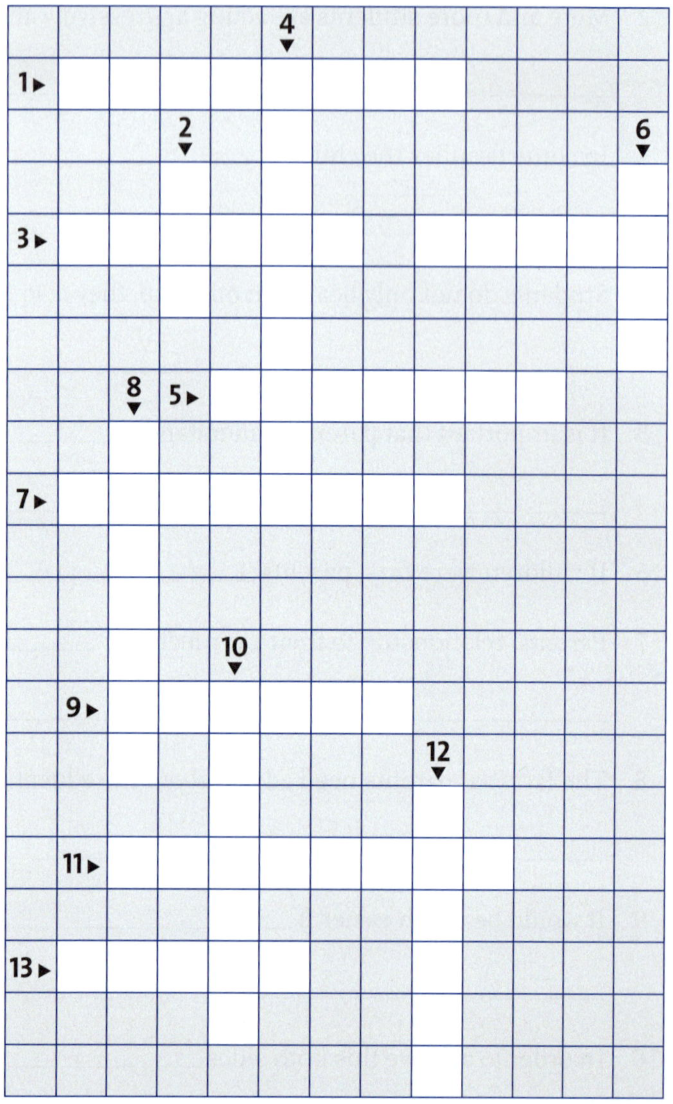

2 GRAMMAR Bollywood

_____/5

Ranjid likes watching Indian movies. This is his e-mail to his German friend Paul in which he tells him about Bollywood films. Shorten the relative clauses using ***present*** *or* ***past participle clauses****.*

Partizipialsätze anstelle von Relativsätzen

- Das Partizip Präsens (**present participle**) bildest du durch das Anhängen der Silbe -ing an den Infinitiv. Im Satz entspricht es einem Relativpronomen (**who**, **which** oder **that**) und einem Verb im Aktiv: the man **who is driving** a car = the man **driving** a car.
- Das Partizip Perfekt (**past participle**) eines regelmäßigen Verbs bildest du durch das Anhängen von **-ed** an den Infinitiv. Im Satz entspricht es einem Relativpronomen (**who**, **which** oder **that**) und einem Verb im Passiv: the car **which is driven** by the man = the car **driven** by the man. Bei unregelmäßigen Verben findest du die Form in der dritten Spalte der Verbliste auf S. 240–241 in deinem Englischbuch.

1 People in Mumbai, who work many hours a day, like light entertainment.

____

2 Many people who wish to spend time with their families often watch Bollywood films on TV.

____

3 Women who watch these movies love the romantic stories and often have a box of handkerchiefs on their knees.

____

____

4 Even in the early days of Bollywood, characters sang in the street and were accompanied by big groups that danced.

____

5 At the end, the hero who wins the girl he loves, kisses her as the crowd dances in the background.

____

____

3 GRAMMAR Meeting a Bollywood star

___/7

Three years ago by chance Ranjid met one of his favourite Indian actors in a cafe in Mumbai. This is his story.

Shorten his sentences using ***participle clauses****. Sometimes you will need to keep a* ***conjunction*** *in front of the* ***participle clause****.*

Partizipialsätze anstelle von adverbialen Nebensätzen

- Partizipialsätze können **Nebensätze der Zeit oder des Grundes** verkürzen. Sie werden in Gesprächen allerdings weniger häufig verwendet.
- Partizipialsätze mit **having + past participle** drücken stets Vorzeitigkeit aus. Wenn du nicht eindeutig erkennen kannst, ob ein Partizipialsatz einen Nebensatz der Zeit oder des Grundes ersetzt, erhalte die **Konjunktion (when, while, after, because, since** ...). Dann ist die Bedeutung klarer.

1 When I walked through the busy streets of Mumbai, I looked into a café at the corner.

____

____

2 After I had walked through the crowded cafe, I found an empty table in a corner.

____

____

3 After he had ordered a hot chocolate, my favourite film star asked me if he could sit at my table.

____

____

4 Since I had just seen his latest movie at the cinema, I asked him all about how it was made.

____

____

5 After I had met him, I went home because I couldn't think about anything else any more.

____

____

6 While I was having dinner, I thought about the afternoon at the café.

____

____

7 The next day I saw my favourite star on TV. He was giving an interview while he was teaching a dancing class.

____

____

MEDIATION

____/12

The forbidden parts of New York City

Im Urlaub hat deine Mutter diesen Handzettel erhalten. Sie bittet dich, ihr zu helfen, weil sie nicht alles genau versteht.

Erkläre, ...
- um was für eine Tour es sich handelt. *(1 fact)*
- was man alles zu sehen bekommt. *(3 facts)*
- was man beachten sollte. *(4 facts)*
- wie viel es kostet.

Mediation längerer Texte
Bei dieser Aufgabe kommt es **nicht** darauf an, wortwörtlich ins Deutsch zu übersetzen. Lies den Text genau und übertrage dann sinngemäß das Wesentlichen ins Deutsche.

Join us for a tour through New York's forbidden boroughs!

**Have they told you not to walk alone through the Bronx?
Have you ever wondered what Central Park looks like at night?
Are you interested in meeting New York gangs?
Have you ever wondered what life is like in a big city after the sun has set?**

Then join us for a tour through the forbidden parts of New York! We'll take the subway and walk you through thrilling Central Park at midnight when all the tourists have long gone home. From the remote hill, you'll have a magnificent view of Manhattan's famous skyline.

Then we'll take the subway again – at night a highlight on its own – to the infamous borough The Bronx. Here you'll get the chance to get up close to a New York gang – if you dare! If it's cold, you can warm yourself by a burning barrel which we will gladly light especially for you.

Then, as the moon starts to set, it'll be time to say goodbye. Let us assure you – you won't be able to sleep that night, even if you make it back to your hotel room!

Please note that this tour is for everybody, however people with heart diseases, pacemakers or high blood pressure should not take part. Don't bring along valuables worth more than $100. Eye catching watches and jewelry should not be worn.

★ Tours start daily at 22.00 hrs.
★ $10 for adults, $5 for under 18s, students and OAPs.

[1] infamous ['ɪnfəməs] *hier: verrucht, verrufen*

Klassenarbeit A

Gesamtpunktzahl ohne Speaking ______ / 87	Note ______
Gesamtpunktzahl mit Speaking ______ / 104	Note ______

LISTENING

______ / 36

10 How social is the social network?

Mr Fitzgerald, a teacher, is looking for a book in the school library. He meets his students Brian and Sarah. Listen to their discussion. Then work on the tasks.

1 Who said what?

______ / 20

a) *Write the numbers of the statements or questions under the photos. Be careful: there are three more statements than you need. (10P)*

Mr Fitzgerald

Sarah

Brian

______ ______ ______

1 Does Facebook have anything to do with faces?

2 It's where people meet other people.

3 Facebook was invented at Harvard University.

4 Obviously it's easy to communicate with people all over the world.

5 I'm keeping in touch with friends I can't see every day.

6 There are certain employers who browse through social networking sites to find out information about the people who work for them.

7 Parents or teachers should surf the net together with children.

8 Young people should be made aware of the dangers linked to social networking sites.

9 If you're careful with your profile, only your friends can access your information and your photos.

10 Spam e-mails are a big problem with the internet.

11 I'm very proud of having 150 Facebook friends.

12 I hope that I will find a boyfriend there.

13 I only use the internet from time to time.

b) *Answer the questions using* ***key words*** *or* ***numbers****. You do not need to write complete sentences. (10P)*

1 What are Brian and Sarah doing in the library?

2 Why does Brian not want Sarah to check her Facebook page?

3 How does Brian explain what Facebook is?

4 What does Mr Fitzgerald think about social networking sites?

5 What is Brian's opinion of social networking sites?

6 What is the danger of social networking sites in Mr Fitzgerald's opinion?

7 How many online friends has Sarah got?

8 Who is Sarah hoping to meet through Facebook?

9 What, in Mr Fitzgerald's opinion, is the advantage of books?

10 How many hours does Sarah usually spend on the computer?

2 Discussing social networking sites

___/ 16

a) *Listen to the conversation again. Write down arguments for and against social networking sites mentioned by Sarah, Brian and Mr Fitzgerald. (6P)*

Pros (+)	Cons (–)

b) *What is your opinion? Add at least* **two** *of your own arguments to the table. (2P)*

c) *How social are social networking sites? Write a short comment of about* **100** *words. (8P)*

LANGUAGE

____/31

1 WORDS You're beautiful, it's true

____/6

Complete the sentences with the correct translation of the German word "schön".

1 Your grandmother always told us what a ______________________ man your grandfather was when he was young.

2 Oh, such a ______________________ baby! How old is she?

3 I think you're the most ______________________ woman I've ever met.

4 Corsica is a ______________________ place to visit in spring.

5 Jim's ______________________, but he knows it and, if you ask me, that doesn't make him so ______________________.

2 WORDS Looking for Mr Right

____/9

In the hope of finding a nice boyfriend, Sarah has posted her profile in an online forum. Complete the text with ***new words from Unit 4****.*

Hi there,

My name is Sarah and I'm talking to all those ______________________ boys out there! I don't like ______________________, so I'm going to ______________________ my thoughts and tell you a bit about myself in a short text. I'm sixteen and still go to school. In my free time I do some ______________________ work. I help old people with their shopping.

I don't mind being single because I've got really great friends, but ______________________ I'm looking for a ______________________. Only write to me if you're serious and looking for a girlfriend. I don't want a boyfriend who will ______________________ me or ______________________ me after a few weeks!

If you think you might be interested, then ______________________ – as a tip I love pizza.

Looking forward to your reply.

Love, Sarah

3 GRAMMAR What will the future bring?

____/ 11

Tim has written a short text about relationships for his school magazine.

Complete the text using the correct ***future tense****.*

Talking about the future
Für das Futur gibt es im Englischen im Wesentlichen drei Möglichkeiten:
- **going to-future**: making plans
- **will-future**: making predictions
- **present progressive**: talking about arrangements, "diary future"

Diese Übung passt zum Grammar File auf S. 162 in deinem Englischbuch.

"____________________ (stay together) when we leave school?" is a question which young people in relationships often ask themselves. You might have spoken to your boyfriend or girlfriend about what you ____________________ (do) after school and it's an important conversation to have. Perhaps you ____________________ (attend) the same university, perhaps you ____________________ (go) to different universities, or one of you ____________________ (stay) at home whilst the other goes away. Whatever happens, your relationship probably ____________________ (not be) the same as it is now.

There are all sorts of questions to answer. How often ____________________ (see) one another? ____________________ (live) together?

These are things which I've been thinking about a lot. Next Monday I ____________________ (meet) my girlfriend, and we ____________________ (discuss) these ideas. I wonder what she ____________________ (say). Luckily there's still some time left before we have to make up our minds.

4 GRAMMAR Simple present for the future

___/5

*Complete the following sentences using the **simple present with future meaning**.*

Ist ein zukünftiges Ereignis in Form eines Fahrplans, Stundenplans oder einem ähnlichen Schema vorgegeben, so wird das **simple present** als **future tense** verwendet.
Verben wie **arrive**, **leave**, **go**, **open**, **close**, **start** oder **stop** können Signalwörter hierfür sein.

1 Josh – ______________________ at 7.30 or 8 o'clock this evening? (the film, start)

2 The Scout soup kitchen ______________________ for the first time this Tuesday. (open)

3 I ______________________ work at 5.30 on Wednesday, so I should be home by 6. (finish)

4 The bus ______________________ at 6.30, so I've got plenty of time to get to work. (leave)

5 What time ______________________ Cologne? (the train, get to)

WRITING

___/20

Social networking sites – an essay

*You have been asked to write an **essay** for the school magazine about the pros and cons of Facebook and other social networking sites. In your text explain what social networking sites are, what you see as their benefits and what the possible negative aspects for users are. Write about **120** words.*

Argumentative writing

- Bei einem argumentativen Text solltest du vor dem Schreiben eine **Gliederung** (**Outline**) erstellen, mit der du deinen Text bereits in Einleitung, deine Argumente und Gegenargumente und Schlussgedanken strukturierst.
- Denke beim Verfassen des Textes auch an **Beispiele**, die deine Meinung oder Auffassung unterstützen. Dies können – sofern vorhanden – auch Ergebnisse von Untersuchungen oder statistische Auswertungen sein. Zum **Schluss** deines Textes wiegst du pro- und contra-Argumente gegeneinander ab und ziehst eine persönliche Schlussfolgerung.
- Weitere Tipps und Beispielgliederungen kannst du im Skills File auf S. 147 oder auf S. 82 in deinem Englischbuch nachlesen.

____

____

____

____

____

____

____

____

SPEAKING

____/17

11 Would you like to go out with me?

There is a new girl at school who has caught Peter's eye. He hasn't talked to her yet, but now she is sitting next to him on the bus and starts a conversation.

Listen to the conversation.

Höre dir das Gespräch ein zweites Mal an und notiere dir nützliche Redewendungen. Sie helfen dir, wenn du dich in **Now you** selbst mit einer Mitschülerin oder einem Mitschüler verabredest. Falls du etwas nicht verstehst, höre dir den Abschnitt noch einmal an. Wenn du mehr Hilfe benötigst, findest du den Hörtext im Lösungsheft auf S. 40.

12, 13 Now you: Asking a girl/boy out

There is a new girl/boy in your class who has caught your eye. You haven't talked to her/him yet, but now she/he is sitting next to you on the bus and starts a conversation.

Talk to her/him by pressing 'pause' when you hear the beep.

Sprechen üben

- Wähle Track 12 oder 13 auf der CD, je nachdem ob du dich mit einem Mädchen oder mit einem Jungen verabreden möchtest.
- Versuche, den Lückendialog möglichst frei zu sprechen.
- Wenn du noch Unterstützung benötigst, nimm deine Notizen zu Track 11 oder dein Englischbuch, S. 83 zur Hilfe.
- Du kannst deinen Dialog aufnehmen und dich so selbst kontrollieren oder deine Eltern und Freunde fragen.
- Vergleiche erst zum Schluss deine Lösung mit dem Lösungsheft.

Gesamtpunktzahl ______ / 59	Note ______

READING

______ / 15

Bono: a celebrity campaigner

1 Hardly any rock star does as much to fight extreme poverty and hunger as the lead singer of the Irish band U2, Bono. Bono cannot accept that, there are countries where people have more money and more to eat than they could ever need, but at the same time there are people in other countries dying of hunger and disease.

2 Bono has said that he became interested in charity work when he watched one of the Secret Policeman's Balls, a charity show organized to raise money for the human rights organization Amnesty International. The first one took place in 1979 with famous comedians and musicians performing on the show for free. In 1986 Bono performed with U2 on an Amnesty International tour of the United States alongside Sting and Bryan Adams. Before that, in 1984, he took part in Bob Geldof's Band Aid project. Band Aid was a group of singers and musicians who raised money for victims of famine by selling a Christmas single called "Do they know it's Christmas?". The project was a huge success.

3 In 1985 Bono and U2 took part in the Live Aid concerts organized by Bob Geldof to raise more money for starving people in Ethiopia. Not long after that Bono and his wife went to Ethiopia to work in an orphanage for several weeks. In the mid-1980s Ethiopia was affected by a serious famine and poverty. The experience shocked Bono and made him determined to work to change the world.

4 Many of U2's songs have political messages, such as the song "Silver and Gold", the B-side to "Where the Streets Have no Name", which was written to support the "Artists United Against Apartheid" project. But besides his music, Bono has used his superstar status to put pressure on political leaders and to encourage them to change policy. For example at the G8 summit in 2005 he and Bob Geldof were allowed to meet US President George W. Bush and the German Chancellor Gerhard Schröder to talk to them about cancelling Third World debt and providing more financial support to Africa. In 2002 he also helped to create DATA, an organization which worked towards a fairer deal for Africa, as well as EDUN, a clothing company, which seeks to encourage trade with Africa. More recently he has founded ONE, an organization which fights extreme poverty and disease.

5 Bono has been nominated for the Nobel Peace Prize, was knighted by the Queen in 2007 and, with Bill and Melinda Gates, was one of TIME magazine's Persons of the Year in 2009.

1 Missing headings

______ / 5

Match the headings A–E to paragraphs 1–5 of the article.

A Awards for his work

B More than just music

C How Bono's campaign work started

D Believe that you can change the world

E A visit to Africa

1		2		3		4		5	

2 About the text

____/ 10

a) *What examples are there in the text of Bono's campaign work? Make notes about at least* ***five*** *things. (5P)*

____

____

____

____

____

b) *Write about* ***50*** *words describing how Bono's campaign work began. (5P)*

____

____

____

____

____

LANGUAGE

____/ 26

1 WORDS A network

____/ 7

a) *Complete the* ***network*** *about charity work. (3P)*

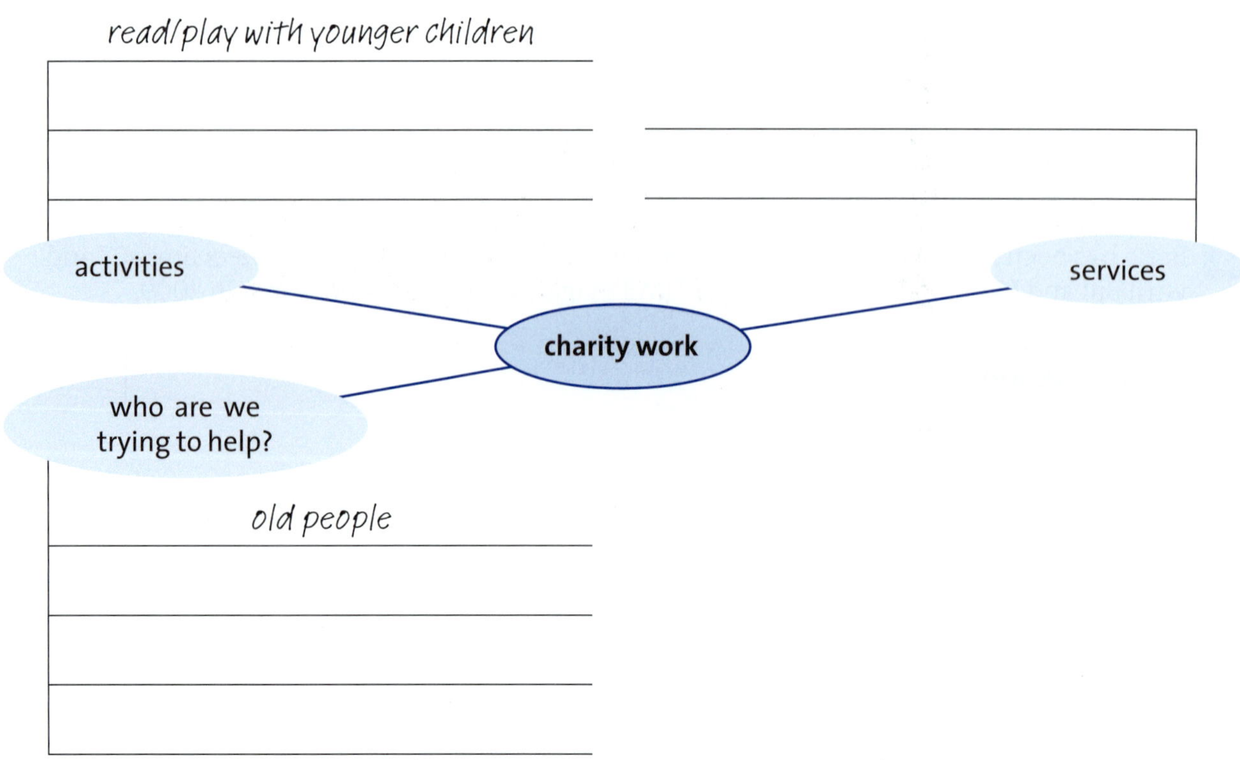

b) *Josh is a member of the Scouts in the United States. His group does a lot for the environment and for people in need.*

*In the following sentences he tells you about the kind of work the Scouts do. Complete the text with words from the network in **a)**. (3P)*

With the Scouts we regularly do ____________________.

One of the things we do every week is ____________________.

The last time we went out we found an old fridge which someone had just left in the woods. And guess what, it still worked!

So we cleaned it up and sold it at a flea market. We decided to ____________________ the money we got to the local ____________________ which provides ____________________ and homeless people with a warm meal, so that they don't go ____________________.

2 WORDS Using new words

____/7

*Complete the text with words from **Unit 4**.*

1 I was playing with my mobile phone as I was walking down the street and I ____________________ a lamppost. How embarrassing!

2 Laura ____________________. She delivers newspapers to the people in my street.

3 Peter likes animals. Yesterday I saw him ____________________ his neighbour's ____________________.

4 David's such a ____________________. He's so polite and always thinks of other people.

5 Gosh, there is a long queue. We'll have to be ____________________.

6 Don't ____________________ to like mathematics. I know you hate it!

7 I don't go out after dark. I'm afraid of ____________________.

3 GRAMMAR An incredible trip

___/6

This summer Sam and Luke stayed with a Spanish host family. During their stay, there were some things they had to do and other things which they were allowed to do.

*Make complete sentences from the notes using **make** or **let** + **object** + **infinitive**.*

1 Clean room ourselves – once a week
2 Stay out until 2 in the morning
3 Use private TV and PC – any time
4 Eat fish or meat – every day
5 Pay €50 extra – day trips
6 Look after baby José – one hour every day

1 ______________________________

2 ______________________________

3 ______________________________

4 ______________________________

5 ______________________________

6 ______________________________

4 GRAMMAR The Scout hut

_____/ 6

Josh and the Boy Scouts have recently moved into a new Scout hut. To get the place ready for their first meeting, they had to prepare a lot of things. The Scouts did many of the jobs themselves, but some had to be done by other people.

Look at the pictures and write sentences using ***have*** *+* ***object*** *+* ***past participle*** *where suitable.*

1 ____

2 ____

3 ____

4 ____

5 ____

6 ____

MEDIATION

____/18

Doing community service

Ahmed is an exchange student at your school. He would like to stay in Germany to do some voluntary community service when he has finished his exchange year. He has done some research about the "Freiwilliges Soziales Jahr", which is open to foreign students if they speak German. However, he doesn't really understand the details of this text from Hesse and needs your help.

Read the website, then ***summarize*** *the text in an e-mail to Ahmed.*

FSJ in Hessen

Viele junge Menschen betreuen Kinder oder hilfebedürftige Menschen und es macht ihnen Spaß. Gehören Sie auch dazu? Oder haben Sie vielleicht schon darüber nachgedacht, wo Sie sich sozial engagieren könnten?

Das Freiwillige Soziale Jahr – FSJ – ist eine solche Möglichkeit. Es bietet jungen Menschen die Chance, bei der Erziehung von Kindern oder der Betreuung von alten und kranken Menschen oder Menschen mit Behinderungen mitzuhelfen – durch persönliche Unterstützung, Begleitung oder Zuwendung. Die jungen Menschen sammeln Erfahrungen, die sie sowohl für den späteren Beruf als auch für das Zusammenleben prägen. Das FSJ ist ein Angebot, das mehr als eine Überlegung wert ist.

Ein Jahr können sich freiwillige Helferinnen und Helfer zwischen 16 und 27 Jahren in einer sozialen, sportlichen oder kulturellen Einrichtung engagieren. Die Einsatzorte reichen von Krankenhäusern über Altenheime bis zu kulturellen und sportlichen Organisationen oder Einrichtungen für Kinder und Jugendliche. Die FSJ-Helferinnen und FSJ-Helfer können sich in Hessen und im Ausland einbringen. Mit dem FSJ kann die Zeit zwischen Schule und Beruf gefüllt werden.

Die FSJ-Helferinnen und FSJ-Helfer bekommen für ihren Einsatz ein Taschengeld, Verpflegung und Unterkunft. Informationen zum FSJ in Hessen sind im Internet unter www.fsj-hessen.de abrufbar. Hier werden alle hessischen FSJ Träger im Kurzprofil vorgestellt – von der Arbeiterwohlfahrt bis zur Katholischen Kirche. So lässt sich schnell feststellen, in welchem Bereich und an welchen Orten man als FSJ-Helferin oder FSJ-Helfer bei den einzelnen Trägern tätig werden möchte. Außerdem findet man hier alle wichtigen Kontaktadressen und Ansprechpartnerinnen und -partner.

How to do well in a test

Countdown zum Testerfolg

Ein Test ist angekündigt? Kein Grund zur Panik. Wichtig ist, dass du weißt, worauf du dich vorbereiten musst. Im Zweifelsfall frag deine Lehrerin oder deinen Lehrer. Der Countdown kann beginnen!

Eine Woche vor dem Test

1 Lies noch einmal die **Texte** der zuletzt durchgenommenen Unit (A-Section und Text, eventuell auch das Background File). Fasse mündlich oder schriftlich zusammen, worum es ging.

2 Wiederhole den **Wortschatz** der Unit mit Hilfe des *Vocabulary* oder des *Wordmaster*.
Schreibe dir die Wörter und Wortverbindungen, die du immer wieder vergisst, auf ein Blatt Papier.
Eine Mindmap oder ein Wortfeld helfen beim Behalten.

3 Geh auch noch mal die neue **Grammatik** durch. Aufgaben zur Selbstüberprüfung und zum Üben findest du im *Practice*-Teil, auf der Seite „How am I doing?", im *Grammar File* (S. 153–166), in deinem *Workbook* und im *e-Workbook*.

Zwei Tage vor dem Test

1 Wiederhole den **Wortschatz**. Manche Wörter sitzen noch nicht? Schreibe einen kurzen Text, in dem du sie verwendest.

2 Lies die **Texte** ein weiteres Mal.

3 Erkläre einem Freund oder einer Freundin die neue **Grammatik**. Das klappt nicht richtig? Dann lies nochmal im *Grammar File* nach.

Am Abend vor dem Test

1 Entspanne dich. Du kannst lesen, dich in die Badewanne legen, Musik hören, fernsehen, ...

2 Geh zur gewohnten Zeit ins Bett.

Am Morgen des Tests

1 Steh rechtzeitig auf, damit du nicht hetzen musst.

2 Lies irgendetwas „zum Aufwärmen", aber schau nicht mehr in dein Schülerbuch.

Während des Tests

1 Denk daran: Du hast dich gut vorbereitet. Es gibt keinen Grund, nervös zu sein.

2 Konzentriere dich auf den Test, lass dich nicht ablenken.

3 Lies dir die Aufgaben genau durch. Dann löse zuerst die Aufgaben, die dir einfach scheinen. Wende dich erst danach den schwereren Aufgaben zu.

4 Aufgaben, die du bearbeitet hast, hakst du ab. So siehst du, wie du vorankommst, und behältst den Überblick.

5 Schau ab und zu auf die Uhr. Du solltest dir für den Schluss noch etwas Zeit einplanen, um deine Antworten noch einmal durchzulesen und wenn nötig zu korrigieren.

Aufgabenstellungen verstehen

Bevor du anfängst, die Aufgaben zu bearbeiten, vergewissere dich, dass du genau weißt, was du tun sollst. Lies die Aufgabe Wort für Wort langsam und gründlich und von Anfang bis Ende durch. Du kannst besonders wichtige Teile der Aufgabenstellung unterstreichen und die Aufgabe, wenn nötig, für dich in einzelne Schritte unterteilen.

Den folgenden Arbeitsanweisungen begegnest du häufig:

Add Verbinde eine Information oder einen Sachverhalt mit einer/einem anderen auf die geforderte Art und Weise.

Choose Wähle zwischen verschiedenen Möglichkeiten die passende Information aus.

Comment Kommentiere einen Sachverhalt durch die Darstellung deiner eigenen Meinung dazu. Begründe und erläutere sie möglichst genau.

Compare Vergleiche Dinge, Wörter oder Sachverhalte, indem du prüfst, ob und auf welche Weise sie gleiche oder verschiedene Eigenschaften, Aussehen, Bedeutungen oder Funktionen haben.

Complete Ergänze eine Information, indem du sie an dem dafür vorgesehenen Platz einträgst und damit z. B. einen Satz sinnvoll beendest.

Describe Beschreibe ein Objekt oder eine Person, d.h. stelle dar, wie sie aussehen, wie das Objekt funktioniert oder die Personen handeln. Vermeide eigene Wertungen wie z. B. „beautiful", „useful" oder „great".

Discuss Diskutiere ein Thema, eine Behauptung oder eine Aussage. Untersuche möglichst viele Seiten davon, z. B. Vor- und Nachteile, und stelle diese geordnet dar.

Explain Erkläre einen Sachverhalt, d. h. gib wesentliche Fakten über ihn und erläutere, wie sie logisch zusammenhängen.

Fill in Trage die geforderten Informationen in den dafür vorgesehenen Platz ein, z. B. in eine Lücke oder eine Tabelle.

List Schreibe einzelne oder mehrere Informationen übersichtlich und geordnet auf, z. B. in einer Reihe, Tabelle oder einem anderen Verzeichnis.

Listen Höre dir einen Text, einzelne Informationen oder Sachverhalte an.

Match Ordne die angegebenen Informationen einander zu, wie es die Aufgabe erfordert. Finde z. B. Satzanfänge und passende Satzenden und füge sie zusammen.

Use Verwende eine Tatsache, ein Wort usw. so, wie es in der Aufgabe gefordert wird.

Write a ... Schreibe etwas in einem geforderten Textformat auf, z. B. deinen Kommentar zu etwas oder eine Geschichte.